let's all
LIVE
better &
LEAD
differently

let's all
LIVE
better &
LEAD
differently

How to Influence and Transform the Cultures Around Us
From the Kitchen Table to the Boardroom and
From Our Communities to Our Nation

RobRoy Walters

Clovercroft Publishing

Published by Clovercroft Publishing, Franklin, Tennessee

The Authorized (King James) Version of the Bible ('the KJV'), the rights in which are vested in the Crown in the United Kingdom, is reproduced here by permission of the Crown's patentee, Cambridge University Press.

Edited by David Brown

Cover Design by Brooke Hawkins

Interior Design by Adept Content Solutions

Printed in the United States of America

978-1-948484-76-3

CONTENTS

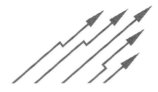

A TRANSFORMATIONAL CONVERSATION

It was around 5:30 in the afternoon when we pulled into the parking lot. My memory of exact dates, from twenty-some years ago, is a little sketchy but my recollection regarding the impact from this event is crystal clear. I was driving a white Ford Taurus sedan with a gray cloth interior. It still had that new car smell. This was a company car provided for my use by the Regional Bank or RB, which is a fictitious name, as are all the names and places used in this book. The events are as real as they get but, as I said in my first book *LIVE better LEAD differently*, I am willing to put myself out to the public but I am not willing to subject others to the same exposure by naming names.

I was RB's controller and I was the mergers and acquisitions (M&A) guy. Actually, I wore a bunch of different responsibility hats during the typical workday, as did most of the executive team at RB. We were a regional bank holding company, located in southeastern Ohio. Our roots in the region were deep and went back almost a hundred years. During the first ninety plus years of the bank's existence, we had grown to around $500,000,000 in assets. It was not large enough to be big, but big enough to start buying up some of the smaller community banks in the area.

I had joined RB about five years earlier as their accounting manager. For those of you who know me from Book 1, you already know that I was a leader in other industries prior to my entry into financial services, and you also know that I subsequently went on to lead several different organizations, from health care to heavy construction. For those of you who don't know me, take a minute and review "Who is Rob?" at the end of this book.

My entry level leadership role within RB soon evolved into serving as the controller of the lead bank, which evolved into being the controller of both the lead bank and the consolidated, holding company. My assuming a lead role in the organization's M&A efforts came about through an interesting turn of events, but we'll save that story for another time. Let's go back to where we left off, pulling into the parking lot.

On this day, our M&A activity had brought me and two other trusted members from the RB team to a small, rural community in southeastern Ohio. The town was located on the Ohio side of the Ohio River and was connected to the state of West Virginia with a narrow, two-lane bridge. As with most downtown parking lots in this part of the country, the lot had been constructed over the vacant ground where a thriving downtown business had once stood. The pavement went right up against a three-story brick wall. You could clearly see the outline of the missing, original structure traced on the wall in front of us. White paint couldn't hide the scars from where the old structure had been demolished, nor did it completely hide the original advertising for the hardware store that had once occupied this site.

It was late spring and about 5:30 in the afternoon. Our meeting was scheduled to start in an hour, which gave us plenty of time to get familiar with the meeting room and set up. The 6:30 start time was chosen so the employees of the branches being acquired from Mega Bank (MB) had time to close their offices and drive to this centrally located site. Our audio/video folks had arrived around 5:00 and were finishing the sound system installation when we walked into the room.

The meeting was being held in an old restaurant/bar located along Main Street. The front of the room was mostly glass and afforded a view of Main Street with the Ohio River flowing by not two hundred yards in the distance. This part of town was prone to flooding just about every spring. Coming from RB, and being located about fifty miles upriver, we understood the beauty of being along the river and the pain associated with living through the spring floods. In the back of the old restaurant was a wooden bar with several high-backed bar stools. The lighting in the room was not great, but it was adequate. We set up the seating for our meeting with the guests' chairs facing the back of the room. A table was placed by the entry where we could register each person as they arrived and provided them with an information packet prepared by RB's human resources department.

As the MB employees began to arrive, Anna and Jill, the two RB team members traveling with me, greeted and registered each guest. I had assumed my usual spot, across the room and away from the activity, so I could watch the body language of the MB employees as they entered the room. Observing their facial expressions and body language, I was looking for any clue regarding their current mindset. The group was clearly tense and apprehensive. You would be too if you had just learned that your workplace was going to be sold to another bank. Who are these people? What happens next? Will I still have a job? All great questions and all questions I was ready to address. Promptly at 6:30, I walked to the front of the group and began what was certain to be an interesting evening.

"Good evening everyone. I am Rob. The first thing I want to do is thank you for being here this evening. Thank you for your time and your attention. Both are valuable and I promise not to waste either.

"I am the controller for RB but, most importantly, you need to know that I am the guy responsible for this meeting. If you want to know who to blame for your world being turned upside down because of this acquisition, you don't have to look any further, it's me (and I held up my right hand above my head). *Don't get angry with your branch managers or your regional manager. All of these discussions took place over the last few months between various executives and me within MB. We are here tonight to answer all your questions as best we can.*

"*Here with me this evening are Anna and Jill. Anna is part of our human resources team and is here to go over the information packet you received when you walked in. Jill leads our conversion team and will be taking care of the conversion process, from converting your deposit customer's balances, to making certain everyone gets replacement checks. Between the three of us, we should be able to address most of your questions this evening.*

"*If we know the answers, we will tell you. We are here to provide you with full transparency regarding any topic that concerns you: your family; your customers; or your branch. If we don't know the answers to your questions, we'll tell you just that; 'we don't know', and we will get back to you with the answer. The phone number, directly into my office, is (xxx) xxx-xxxx, and my company cell number is (xxx) xxx-xxxx. I am available, any time, to everyone: employees, customers, and shareholders. You will find my numbers, as well as Anna's and Jill's direct numbers, listed on the second page of the packet you received when you walked in.*

"*Just as we will answer all of your questions to the best of our ability, we will also tell you if the subject you are asking about is none of your business. We are both (MB and RB) SEC registered, publicly traded companies. Some of the details related to this transaction are not public information and need to remain confidential. It is just that simple. We will tell you whatever we know and when we can't give you the answer, we will tell you that too.*

"*I know this level of transparency is not what you are accustomed to, but for RB, it is part of who we are. We are not just providing financial services to these markets; we are part of our communities. This area is our home. RB's culture has evolved over the last ninety years to reflect the culture of the people we serve. That is one of the reasons we have been so successful. We have constructed a business model that has respect at its core. We respect the needs of our customers, our shareholders, and our team members, and these elements form the core of RB's culture.*

"*I like things simple and, as you have already figured out, I like to be straightforward. If you want to know something, just ask me. One of the questions I get most often during these types of meetings is: 'What is it like to work at RB?' That is a great question and here is the best way I have found to answer that question: 'There are three rules you must remember at all times, only three. Rule #1 is to be professional, which begins with respect for the customer, your team members, and yourself. Rule #2 is to work smarter, not harder. How many hours you work doesn't impress me at all. What you have accomplished during those hours is what matters. And Rule #3, maintain balance in life; have fun!'*

"That's it. Pretty simple. I know you have a bunch of questions this evening, so let's start with Anna and she will cover the HR packets in front of you. After Anna covers the HR material, Jill will give you a brief description of how the conversion process works and what your customers will need to know. After they go over their materials for this evening, we will open the discussion up to your questions. You can ask anything that is on your mind and we will do our best to give you the answer.

"Anna, the floor is yours. Oh, by the way folks, Anna and Jill are good people. They know their pieces in this process very well. I respect them and I trust their judgment, and you can too. Anna..."

With that being said, I handed the mic to Anna and sat down on one of the bar stools. She spent about thirty minutes going over the prepared HR materials. Jill's presentation followed. It was shorter and very broad in scope. She took about fifteen minutes to give the group an outline of how the process would work and an approximate timeline for the conversion.

Anna was the consummate HR professional. She had a natural ability to project both understanding and empathy. Her tone and demeanor were always reassuring and she had the anticipated calming effect on the group. Anna was the go-to person in HR. If you wanted to get something done, see Anna. She never wanted the spotlight, which worked well because her boss was one who was always in search of center stage. This was our second or third M&A presentation together and our largest group to date. As we worked through the various M&A presentations, Anna's skills had grown rapidly and, on this particular evening, she knocked it out of the park. By far, this was her best presentation. She immediately connected with the audience and kept their attention for the entire thirty minutes.

When Jill took the floor, the group was fully engaged. They had entered the room this evening with a clear and understandable chip on their shoulders. So far, we had been true to our word. Out of respect, we had not wasted their time, nor was their attention going unrewarded. Jill did her usual great job. She had an interesting backstory, one worth exploring.

I had discovered Jill during our first M&A conversion. She was squirrelled away in a small cubicle in the loan processing department. She had been recently hired to do data entry related to the conversion of loans from an earlier acquisition. What brought me to Jill's office? I was in search of answers to ongoing process problems related to one of RB's earlier conversions. This M&A conversion was not going as well as we had hoped. On this particular day, I was trying to get an answer to what I thought was a straightforward question. Unfortunately, I was being stonewalled by everyone I spoke with.

People being people, sometimes these things happen. When I encounter resistance in obtaining needed information, I find it more effective to pay the area holding my interest (the information I need) a personal visit. I learned long ago that it is always harder to tell me "No" when someone is looking me in the eyes, as opposed to talking with me over the phone. Anyway, my first stop was to see the director of the area. She did not have the answer (which I already knew) but she directed me to a person who might know. At this point in time, the director's only concern was to get me out of her office and shift my attention to someone else. That lucky person happened to be Jill.

When I walked around the corner toward Jill's workspace, there were two team members standing outside her cubicle and a third was inside. As they caught sight of me headed their way, they started shuffling their feet. It was easy to see that my unexpected presence made them uncomfortable. After all, what was a "suit" doing in this area? (All male RB team members wore at least a sport jacket and tie. However, all male executives wore suits every day. It was part of the RB culture.) No executive ever came into this area unless there was a real problem, which meant someone in the loan processing department was in trouble.

The two ladies standing outside of Jill's office offered up a nervous greeting: *"Good morning, Mr. Walters."* Using a more formal greeting was also part of the RB culture, one which I was on a mission to change. *"Good morning, ladies and please, it is Rob. When someone calls me Mr. Walters, I start looking over my shoulder to see if my dad is standing there."* One of the team members asked if they could help me, and I responded by letting them know that I had been sent by the director to see Jill. *"I just have a couple of quick questions,"* I said as they both excused themselves and disappeared into the maze of cubicles. As I stepped into Jill's work area for the first time, I realized that Jill, the newly hired employee, was leading a long-time RB employee through a complex section of the loan conversion process. They immediately stopped what they were doing. The look on the other person's face was one of sheer panic. She was trapped in a cubicle by a suit, with no way out. I apologized for the interruption and encouraged them to continue. I offered to come back at a more convenient time, which was met with the predictable: *"Oh no, Mr. Walters, we were just wrapping up."* I responded: *"Good timing then, and please, it's Rob."*

Jill turned around and looked me straight in the eyes. *"How can I help you, Rob?"* Her question and her demeanor offered no hesitation and established no limits. These were words spoken by someone who had obviously been spending much of her time teaching others, which was amazing to me considering the complexity of the topic and the fact that she had only been with RB for less than a year. I sat down and asked my questions. The subject of my questions is long forgotten, but the manner in which she responded has stayed with me. Jill not only knew the answers, but she explained *how* the process worked and *why* it worked that way. She could explain, in terms that I understood, the entire flow of the information related to my topic.

It quickly became clear to me that the two ladies standing outside of her cubicle were not standing there to shoot the bull. They were standing there to learn. I had learned a lot in a short period of time with Jill. Not only did I get the answers to my questions, but I had found someone with a skill set which was desperately needed within the M&A team. I had also learned that we needed a new director to lead the loan processing area. Jill would become the person that would transition into filling both of those roles.

Rolling time forward from Jill's backstory and rejoining our presentation to the MB group, Jill had wrapped up her overview, and it was now time to open the floor to questions from the group. I stood up and turned off the mic. Previous experience had taught me that speaking without a microphone in small groups like this one serves to make the conversation more personal; plus, it forces the audience to focus more intently on what is being said. It is much like when people naturally strain to hear a whisper but ignore someone who is shouting. My voice carries well, and I had developed the habit of repeating the questions being asked. The key is to make certain everyone can hear the questions being asked and the answers being given. I had taken my suit jacket off and loosened my tie, signaling to the group that it was time to get down to business.

"Let's get started. What is on your mind?" was my invitation to the group to start the Q&A session. I was waiting for one question in particular. It was the reason I was here for this meeting. Up to this point, other than providing a name and a face for them to blame for their world being upended, Anna and Jill had delivered all of the useful information. I didn't have to wait long. After an awkward minute or two of silence within the group, here it came. They asked the question I had been waiting to hear: *"Am I going to lose my job?"*

Being that this particular question was the first one out of the box told me that we had been successful in establishing the beginnings of a relationship with this group. We had been able to establish a sense of trust, project integrity, and successfully communicate our message (the three elements necessary for establishing any form of relationship). Now came the moment for me to contrast myself and, by extension, to contrast the RB culture from the MB culture. My answer was clear and to the point, which shocked the assembled group and clearly took Anna by surprise. I queried back: *"Is your job in the proof department?"* The individual answered back in a loud, clear voice with a challenging tone: *"Yes, I work in the proof department and so do a bunch of us here tonight. Will we still have our jobs?"* (The "proof department" was the area of the bank that scans and posts all of the non-electronic transactions processed by the bank on a daily basis. The area requires exacting work, and it is critical for the work to be completed in a timely manner.)

"No." I answered in a definitive but empathetic tone. *"If you are employed in the proof department, about four months after the acquisition is complete, all proof functions will be consolidated into one of our existing proof departments."* (FYI: one of the existing proof operation centers was about thirty minutes away from where we were meeting, and the other was about an hour away. Either center could absorb the MB workflow.)

There was an audible grumbling which rose up from the group and an immediate exchange of inaudible comments between the folks in the audience. After about thirty seconds had passed, a young man seated toward the back of the room stood up and in a clear voice began to address me: *"Mr. Walters, Rob, I am Tim, the manager of the ABC Branch, and the people employed in the proof department are my employees. We have been told that no one was going to lose their job as a result of MB selling these branches to RB. Now you are telling us that we are going to lose our jobs! What are we supposed to believe?"*

"Did everyone hear Tim's comments and question?" I asked the group. The group responded with a collective "yes," so I continued. *"Thank you, Tim for your honesty and for respecting those you work with enough to stand up on their behalf. I know that wasn't easy for you to do."* I paused long enough to drag my stool, separating it from Anna and Jill, and placing it in the center/front of the group. The act of separating my stool from Anna and Jill was intentional and designed to focus the discussion that was about to take place on one, and only one person, me.

Again, holding up my right hand above my head, I began: *"As I said earlier, I am the guy responsible for turning your world upside down. When I say that I am responsible, I mean that I am the guy who negotiated with MB's executive team establishing the terms and conditions of this transaction. I actually drafted much of the language in the legal documents that govern this transaction and I am responsible to RB's board and shareholders for the actual results from our future together. No one person knows the details of this deal better than I, and no one has more tied to its future success, or failure, than I. So, believe me when I tell you that there was never a representation from RB that the proof department would remain in operation, post closing. In fact, during the negotiations, I made it very clear that it is and was always our intention to merge your proofing functions with the existing RB proof departments."* At this point, you could have heard a pin drop in the room. As you can imagine, the entire group was fully engaged.

At that moment, a random comment was aired by someone in the group: *"So they lied to us again."* I immediately responded with: *"I doubt it. It's possible, but I imagine it is more likely a miscommunication occurred somewhere between the MB executives that negotiated this deal and the MB manager that delivered the message. This type of thing happens all the time. I apologize for the confusion, but that is why we are talking this evening. We are here to answer your questions and address any concerns you may have. My main objective for this evening was to get to this discussion regarding the future of the proof department. May I take just a few minutes to share with you how and why these decisions were made?"*

I continued: *"You and I are all in this together. If this goes badly, it is my fault and my fault alone. If our efforts are successful, you are the folks that made it happen, and you will get all of the credit. Let me share just a brief snapshot of our vision of what we can accomplish for our customers and the communities we serve...."*

With those words being spoken, a calm settled over the group and, for the first time in a long time, they felt like they were going to become part of a team. They had an opportunity to help shape their own futures. They had been given something they had not expected, that being the honesty that comes from respect combined with a clear sense of purpose. I went on to explain to the group that no one involved in direct customer contact would be displaced. I also explained that, within the business model which we used to project the financial results from their region over the next eighteen months, we had built in the cost of hiring additional branch employees. This brought a collective comment from the group: *"Thank heavens. We are _way_ understaffed in the branches."* I also shared with them RB's use of technology. We had spent the last few years building what was, for that point in time, a new type of data management system. RB's systems were designed to put the power of technology in the hands of the end user and take it out of the hands of the backroom, mainframe programmers. I challenged them to learn these new concepts quickly because we had found that, with this new power in the hands of the frontline employees, customers were very pleased with the improved flexibility and speed of service. Our leveraging technology to better serve our customers had been the reason why RB was able to quickly grow its market share. We had grown, not because of price, but due to the quality of service (value) being delivered to the customer.

As we were wrapping up the meeting, I added: *"I want to make this one final point. We have a challenging four or five months ahead of us. There will be problems and you will become frustrated. Call me whenever you need to, but more importantly, talk with each other. Help each other. For those of you who choose to leave, I certainly understand and will support you any way I can. If you choose to stay with us over the next six months, there will be a retention bonus. Anna will be able to give you the details. For those of you in the proof department, you will be given strong consideration for any positions that open up in the branches and in RB's existing proof departments. If you are employed as a proof operator and stay with us during this transaction, you will receive a severance package as part of your termination, which will be based on your accumulated years of service. Is that fair?"* The answer came back in the form of smiles from the group and an audible, collective murmur of *"yes"* and *"thank you."*

"Thank you for your time and attention this evening. I am looking forward to working with each of you. We will stay around for a little while if you have any questions. Please be safe going home. Good night." And with that, the presentation ended. In total, we spent around ninety minutes in front

of the MB group. The lines for questions formed immediately but very few questions were directed toward me. The MB folks wanted to talk to Anna and Jill. This reaction was the best I could have hoped for. This mix of follow-up questions was a clear indication that their focus was on the future. They wanted to know what came next and, most importantly, how they could help. A wonderful result!

I received a few handshakes and the customary *"thank you for being here"* comments, but two post-presentation conversations stand out in my mind. The first was a young lady who was obviously upset but had the strength to come up and share her life-challenging circumstances (a single mother with a small child). It had been hard for her to find work. The evening hours worked by the proof department matched with her needs perfectly. She had no idea what she was going to do, but she knew she wanted to work for me (RB). Her question was basically: *"What do I need to learn to get a job in the branch?"* She committed to stay through the entire process because she felt that was the right thing to do. The young lady was true to her word. She never missed a day's work through the conversion. And yes, she was hired at one of the branches. She was successful at keeping her job, not because of anything I had done, but because of what she had done. She earned it.

The second memorable conversation was with Tim, the branch manager, who had spoken up earlier on behalf of this team. Tim was part of the local community, born and raised. He was well-educated and well-spoken. He was raising his young family in his hometown and wanted to talk more about our plans for the future. What would this mean to his customers, his community, and his team? Clearly, this guy was a winner! He had been shunned by the leadership of MB because of his direct approach to asking pointed questions and his passion for the area. I had been warned about this gentleman from the MB team. As far as MB was concerned, he had proven to be a problem, a real trouble-maker, but not in my world! Tim was the type of leader I was looking for. Long story made short, about a year later, we were ready to hire a regional manager to oversee all of the branches in the area. The regional vice president from MB applied, and I interviewed him. He didn't get the job. Tim became RB's new regional manager. Tim had earned the opportunity and went on to continued success within RB.

What else came out of that meeting? Well, there were several additional points of interest from that evening. When we got in the car to drive home, no one said anything for a little while. Then I asked: *"Well, how do you think that went?"* Jill spoke first and commented on all she had learned about their existing systems. She was shocked by how far behind MB was in the application of new technology. Jill saw this as a great opportunity to help the new employees to better serve their customers. After a few minutes, Jill buried herself into her work, but Anna remained strangely quiet. I said, *"Anna, you're not saying much. What do you think?"* To my surprise, Anna's voice cracked with emotion: *"Thank you for what you did back there. I have never seen anything like it. They will never know the risks you are taking on their behalf."*

Jill was in the back seat working away as Anna spoke. When she heard those words, her eyes shot up and immediately focused on Anna. This was our second trip together related to a pending M&A conversion, but Jill didn't quite yet grasp what had taken place. From her workspace in the back seat, Jill raised the questions: *"What risk, Anna? What are you talking about?"*

Anna turned to me to see if I was going to respond. I simply said: *"Go ahead."* With that, Anna began explaining to Jill that the accepted practice in a conversation of this type was to always avoid direct answers to direct questions. Also, she had never seen anyone commit to taking responsibility for future results, much less taking responsibility in advance for all those things that would almost certainly go wrong during the course of something as complicated as an acquisition and the related conversion.

Then, there were the political risks I had just taken. RB's culture had been one of centralized control and closely held information. What I shared with this group was well beyond RB's accepted cultural norms. Anna was shocked by what she had heard and was worried about the possible consequence to me. *"Do you know what you have done? Do you know how Terry will react to this?"* (Terry is how we will refer to the EVP of HR, a major force within the existing RB leadership structure.) Anna continued: *"What am I going to tell Terry in the morning when he asks about how the meeting went tonight?"* I responded: *"Anna, tell Terry exactly what happened this evening. Don't leave out any details. Tell him what you saw, what you heard, and especially tell him how you felt. Answer any questions he may have and encourage him to talk to me. I would love to have a conversation with him regarding tonight's meeting."* *"Oh, he won't come to see you,"* she warned. *"He will go straight to Mr. E. and tell him what happened."* (Mr. E. is the abbreviation we are using to represent the long-serving President and CEO of RB.) *"I am counting on it,"* I said with a smile. That was all Anna needed. *"You have covered your bases, haven't you? Are we headed in a new direction, Rob?"* she asked. *"Yes,"* I responded. And before I could start into a deeper explanation, Anna wisely cut me off and said: *"I don't need to know and don't want to know anything else. Thank heavens! We have needed to change our culture for years. I liked what I saw tonight."* Anna lowered her voice to almost a whisper and said: *"Thank you for what you are doing, but be careful."* With that, she turned her head to the side window and spent most of the remaining trip back to the office in silence.

Jill had listened to the conversation, but at this point in her development, she was not politically attuned nor was she the least bit interested in corporate politics. "Get it done!" was Jill's singular focus. She would later become skilled in viewing the cultural horizon from both a systemic and a political perspective. For that night, she had given up trying to work in the dark and sat in silence the rest of the way back.

So many of my life lessons are rooted in events like this one. What makes them memorable? The emotion. The intense focus of the moment. The ability to recall with clarity a point in time where I was in the position to make a difference, learn a valuable lesson, or discover a truth. Each of these memorable lessons have helped me to develop the materials I shared with you in Book 1 and those I am about to share with you now.

Before moving on to lessons learned, let's close the circle regarding the events which began that evening. The acquisition of the MB branches took place on schedule and went smoothly. All of the representations I made to the group that night were kept, and out of about a dozen MB employees employed in the proof department, only a couple received a severance package. The rest were employed by RB in the branches. The transaction was a success for our customers, our shareholders, and our culture. The financial pro forma models which had been constructed and formed the basis for our pricing for the transaction, projected that the purchase would become accretive to RB's shareholders (we would start making money on our initial investment) within eighteen months. We were making money by the end of the first year and profits accelerated each quarter thereafter for several quarters. Deposit volumes exceeded projections and the average cost of funds generated from the new market stayed well within the projected ranges. Customer counts increased along with the ratio of relationships per customer. The facilities were quickly renovated and the new technologies were put to work assisting our team members in helping our customers. By all measures and appearances, this acquisition was a success.

Anna's concerns regarding the political repercussions toward me were well founded. The next day was indeed filled with fireworks that went on behind closed doors between Terry and Mr. E. I had won that battle on that day. I won the moment because the people I was responsible to (RB's "Core": our customers, our shareholders, and our culture) were all going to benefit from our short-term and long-term gains. All was good on that day and for many days to follow. In fact, the next couple of years were filled with several victories on the cultural battlefield, and as a result of a strong team effort, RB was succeeding beyond all expectations.

As for me, I had assembled a strong team around me, and developed an excellent relationship with our board of directors and with several key RB shareholders. We would expand into several new markets, branching over into the state of West Virginia. RB's strategic footprint was focused on further expansion north into central Ohio, and west into the Commonwealth of Kentucky.

Aside from the support I received from the CEO and the board, the RB executive team had accepted that I viewed things differently, and in their own way, they had learned to tolerate me. As shareholders themselves, they had learned that this new culture stuff was increasing the value of their RB shares and, as a result, increased their own personal net worth. So, for now, folks were willing to go along with the new direction. Patience is a virtue, and in this case, tolerating the new culture was becoming quite profitable for everyone. From where the RB executive team sat, why not go along? There would always be time to win the war later, when the opportunity presented itself.

I was still in my mid-thirties. My wife and I had recently completed construction on a new home (which she had designed from the ground up). It was located just down the street from her parents, directly across from a beautiful city park and the elementary school she had attended while growing up. The next year, our son would start attending kindergarten at that same school. I was learning every minute of every day. I was doing what I loved: being a husband and a father; helping to build a company; leading cultural transformation; and teaching night courses at a local college. Life was great, jam-packed, but great!

Events, some of which I will share with you during the discussion of human *choices* and *needs*, were about to unfold that would lead to my promotion to president and CEO of a new banking company. Just about a year later, my family and I would relocate to northeastern Kentucky. These changes would open up a whole new world of opportunities and challenges, testing my strength of character and teaching me invaluable life lessons. Life is a wonderful teacher. Never stop learning!

INTRODUCTION

Out of the many life experiences I have had, why did I choose this event to set the stage for this book? Because, in retrospect, it frames so many life lessons learned, and it represented a pivotal point in my development as a leader. I began my career by first learning to work *for* people. Those talents served me well until the age of nineteen when I entered into my first leadership role. As an entry level leader, I needed to acquire the knowledge necessary to work both *for* and *with* people. I would go on to learn that developing the knowledge necessary to work *with* people is tied directly to my ability to build and maintain productive relationships.

Once I had acquired the basic knowledge of leadership (leadership being defined as the ability to influence others), the next hurdle was to test my knowledge in as many different settings as possible and grow from each experience. Basically, I needed to <u>learn</u>. Eventually, my knowledge developed into a set of skills. Testing these skills over and over again generated a level of understanding which enabled me to conduct meetings like the one relived in "A Transformational Conversation" above. Ultimately these skills and understanding helped me to learn how to effectively influence (transform) cultures.

The paragraphs above contain so much information and so many opportunities for us to learn that it actually serves well as an overview for: <u>let's all LIVE better & LEAD differently </u>(Book 2). It is at this point in the creative process where I need to strike a balance between the needs of those who have already read: <u>LIVE better LEAD differently</u> (Book 1). Book 1 was written with a focus on learning both the "how" and "why" of leadership, understanding the foundations for human development, personal growth, and productive relationships. The experiences for the reader contained in Book 1 are applicable to both individuals and populations.

Book 2 picks up the concepts, tools, and techniques from Book 1 and takes them to the next level. Within Book 2, we pull back the shroud of mystery surrounding cultural change to reveal that leadership/influence, in all of its forms, applies equally to an individual or a population. We take the major themes from Book 1 and advance our knowledge regarding the topics of: The Relationship Model; the power of changes in perception and perspective; The Cycle of Human Development; and several new concepts and models.

During our journey, we will progress from understanding the construction of productive relationships, one of the major focuses within Book 1, to learning the "how" and "why" behind cultural change, which is the primary focus of this second book. The concepts and models that were introduced in Book 1, and used again in Book 2, have been identified and then briefly summarized before being expanded upon. If you desire a more complete understanding of these Book 1 carryovers, I would encourage you to purchase Book 1. There is much more within the pages of <u>LIVE better LEAD differently</u> for you to learn than just the carryover concepts.

Let's begin our journey through Book 2 by plowing some new ground. We start by defining a word that we all use frequently. The word "culture" is similar to the words "good" or "true." All of these words, and many more that we reference every day, have become subject to an individual's interpretation. Within these pages, we will learn the practical meaning of these words and many more that are central to the leadership process. We will explore the "how" and "why" behind their meanings and learn, as leaders, to first understand and then teach others their application. We begin with culture.

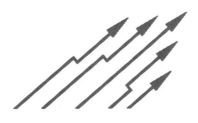

Life Question #1
WHAT IS CULTURE?

So, what is a culture? First, cultures exist everywhere. As the subtitle to this book would indicate, you will find cultures: ".... From the Kitchen Table to the Boardroom and From Our Communities to Our Nation." When two or more individuals (a population) gather together, wherever that gathering may occur, you have the makings of a culture. Second, a culture is a population which shares a set of collective *choices* and *needs*. And finally, this set of cultural *choices* and *needs* is the product of interactions between three internal and three external cultural influences.

The three internal cultural influences are trust, integrity, and communication. Cultures are also shaped by three external influences, which are environmental conditions, economic conditions, and expectations. In short, cultures are formed when a population shares a set of experiences within similar environmental and economic conditions, which are subject to imposed expectations. Simply stated, "culture" is a collective relationship. Cultures are transformed by influences, be they internal or external. Therefore, cultures are subject to transformation through the skillful application of the tools used in relationship management (the focus of Book 1).

> *Culture is a collective relationship.*

In every productive relationship existing between a population of two or two hundred million, influences are balanced on the other party's individual or collective point of perception. Influence is granted as a direct result of the population's perception of trust and integrity placed in the leader. These first two relationship elements are supported by a foundation created from the third relationship element, which is substantive communication. Within the boundaries of any relationship, there are three catalysts which are in constant circulation, maintaining the strength of the productive relationship elements. These catalysts are emotion, purpose, and substance, as shown in Illustration #1 below: The Relationship Model.

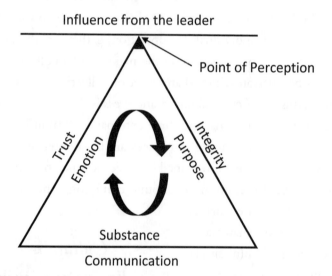

A productive relationship functions much like the human body. Catalysts are moving constantly within the framework of the relationship, caring for and strengthening the three elements which give emotion (trust) and purpose (integrity) to the relationship. These catalysts are much like our blood which circulates constantly tending to the health of our cells. The result of a well-maintained circulatory system is a body with the ability to continue its functions and accomplish its purposes. When the internal circulatory system fails, the body fails. When the internal catalysts of a productive relationship fail, one or more of the elements will fail and the relationship ceases to be productive.

While the catalysts serve a critical function, forming the internal influences impacting the relationship, the three elements (trust, integrity, and communication) form the protective boundaries of a relationship. These three elements enable the relationship to withstand the external forces of change. The external forces of change are being levied on the relationship by environmental and economic conditions, as well as the imposition of expectations. The two-dimensional Relationship Model is evolving into a more advanced, three-dimensional Culture Model as shown in Illustration #2 below: **The Culture Model**.

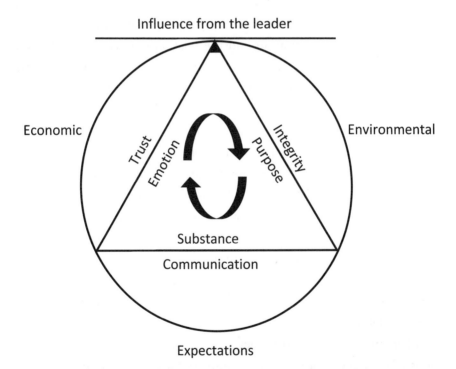

Visualize the Culture Model as a globe surrounding the Relation-ship Model. Now that we are mentally visualizing a three-dimensional illustration, we should adjust our view of the Relationship Model and realize it actually exists in the form of a pyramid. The visualization of a four-sided equilateral triangle, a pyramid structure, provides a new perception of the relationship, giving it a more appropriate level of strength and stability. We now view the relationship as having more internal areas to be tended by the circulating catalysts. The three elements (trust, integrity, and communication) form a substantial barrier which extends in all directions, shielding the internal functions of a relationship from the ever-changing external forces which surround it. External influences are in a state of constant rotation around the relationship. Much like Earth's global wind currents and weather patterns, the external environmental and economic conditions acting on the culture are shifting constantly.

The external environmental and economic conditions acting on culture are shifting constantly

Rob: *"You have just defined a culture as a collective relationship that is in a constant state of change. How on Earth can you lead the transformation of a collective relationship that is always changing?"* Answer: "… how on Earth …" What a great way to pose the question. How on Earth, indeed. Let's make the intangible tangible by associating it with something we all know and use every day. How do we predict the weather? How on Earth can meteorologists monitor hurricanes, predicting one of Mother Nature's most powerful and unpredictable forces? Today's computer-based models can project, with amazing accuracy, a hurricane's strength, speed, direction, and even, in most cases, the time and place of their landfall well in advance of the actual event. We routinely check the weather apps on our smartphones and have learned to trust the projections of the daily conditions being displayed for our community or the region to which we are flying.

"How on Earth…?" The answer to your cultural question has the same basic structure as the answer to the meteorologist's question. Meteorologists use predictive modeling developed with the use of sophisticated tools and honed by years of results. As leaders, we apply our own predictive models, combined with our use of leadership tools, which are also improved through experienced results. Successfully leading the transformation of a collective relationship depends heavily on the quality of the data being extracted and quality of the tools used to process the data into information.

When it comes to the quality of the present facts being searched (data), the old saying is as true today as it was forty years ago: "Garbage in. Garbage out." That means the quality of the data resulting from the search of flawed or incomplete present facts can never exceed the quality of the facts being selected against. Flawed facts equate to flawed data. Flawed data being processed by the most sophisticated informational tools known to man will always produce flawed information. Think of it this way, when you search through a massive pile of garbage, no matter how quickly your search engine affects the selection process, you are going to end up selecting garbage. This is why the Cycle of Human Development (the Cycle) begins with the Universe of Present Facts, and every time we loop back to refresh our data, we are re-testing our facts. This Cycle is also how we all learn and develop. The more times curiosity leads us to re-test our Present Facts, the more likely new facts, previously undiscovered facts, will migrate over from the Universe of Absent Facts and become part of the present. Understanding the migration process of facts and especially understanding the barrier which exists between Present and Absent Facts, is one of the cornerstones of cultural transformation. We will explore migration influences when we dive into ideology versus results in Life Question #4.

We now turn our attention to the use of informational tools. Informational tools enable us to place into context the data being presented for processing. In short, data placed in context by tools allows us to anticipate the result of the information when it is applied. The more frequently we correctly anticipate the result of the applied information, the more we trust the quality of the data being gathered. The Culture Model, Illustration #2, is one of two critical tools used by leaders to understand culture, placing into context the external and internal influences at work within any collective relationship.

The second tool, which is critical to the development of the leader's predictive skills, is the Cycle of Human Development.

Cycle of Human Development

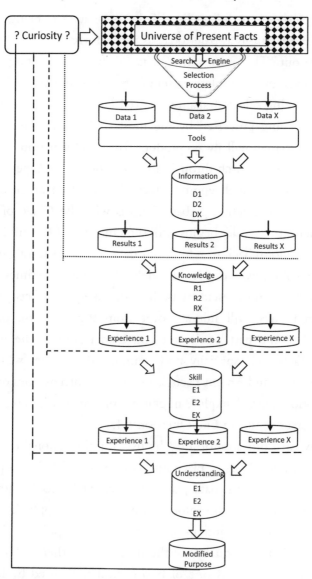

As you review the Cycle (Illustration #3 above), notice that human development begins with the "Universe of Present Facts." Present Facts are those that are both current and existing. Within the context of the Cycle, current simply means readily available to you through some type of automated or manual discovery process. The facts which exist and are accepted today may be replaced or disproven tomorrow.

Just because facts are present does not make them accurate

Facts change as knowledge evolves. The key takeaway point to consider is, just because facts are present (discovered) does not make them accurate. Like the weather, Present Facts constantly change, as do the tools we use to predict future conditions. Hold on to this basic understanding of present, discoverable facts. We will be combining this concept with our exploration of the "Universe of Absent Facts" (undiscovered facts).

Between our discussion of facts, data, and tools (The Culture Model and the Cycle of Human Development), we have addressed the foundational answer to Life Question #1: "What is culture?" **Culture is a collective relationship which is subject to development based on external and internal influences.** These influ-

Once you learn to predict cultural development you can influence its growth

ences, when placed in proper context through the use of tools, make cultural development predictable. Once you learn to predict cultural development, you can influence its growth, which generates the opportunity for leading cultural transformation.

On to the next logical Life Question: "How do cultures learn and develop?"

Life Question #2
HOW DO CULTURES LEARN AND DEVELOP?

When I walked into the meeting with the MB employees, I walked in with a developed set of leadership skills. For years, I had been a student of leadership, learning every day from experience, observation, and research. At the age of thirty-five, I had the advantage of sixteen years of experience in learning and applying my leadership skills. I had a solid understanding of how to influence (to lead) individuals as well as groups. Two keys to my success in leadership were the ability to communicate a clear vision for the future, combined with an unshakable commitment to purpose.

Two keys to success in leadership are the ability to communicate a clear vision and an unshakable commitment to purpose.

When I stepped in front of the assembled MB team, I was prepared. I had a good grasp of the environmental and economic conditions which existed within the MB culture. This informational context allowed me to predict their expectations, and therefore, I was prepared to answer the questions asked by the group. I was able to anticipate their questions because I had spent endless hours working to discover the facts that were, in the beginning, absent from my knowledge regarding MB. To prepare for this meeting, I had taken what I had discovered about MB and combined it with my understanding of how individuals and cultures develop (the Cycle). In other words, my *choice* of curiosity had led me to test and re-test my information about MB, developing new and additional information each time I looped back to the beginning of the Cycle.

Based on my understanding of productive relationship management, I knew that it was critical for me to invest the time, in advance of the meeting, to understand the nature of the choices and needs of the individuals that would be seated in front of me. In addition, I was confident in my own choices and needs and understood well those of the RB groups I represented: customers, shareholders, and culture. These three groups formed my **Core of Responsibility** (the **Core**). In short, I had invested the time necessary to understand the current condition of the MB culture, and I was able to anticipate the *choices* and *needs* of the culture I was about to transform.

Doing the necessary work up front is just a starting point. Knowing where to invest your time requires a different set of skills. The questions you may be asking are: "How did I know what to focus on in order to prepare?" and "How was I able to anticipate the questions from the group?" Both are great questions and deserve an in-depth answer.

> *Customers, shareholders and culture form a leader's Core of Responsibility*

Let's address your questions by going back to our broader question: "How do cultures learn and develop?" We will find some answers by continuing our study of the Cycle of Human Development (shown in Illustration #3). After learning more about how the Cycle functions, we will find additional answers by exploring the concepts surrounding human *choices* and *needs*. We will wrap up our discussion of Life Question #2 by introducing the concept of the Core and the role it plays in the cultural transformation process.

Cultural Learning and Development:
The Cycle of Human Development

The Cycle of Human Development always begins within the Universe of Present Facts. The entire body of Present Facts can be accessed through either automated or manual search engines. Please note that my use of the term "search engine" is nothing more than an attempt to modernize the age-old process of learning from the world around us. Staying within that same school of thought, the use of the phrase "Universe of Present Facts" is my way of illustrating the vast body of known facts available through the use of search engines, both automated and manual.

Examples of automated search engines would be Google, Bing, etc. You get the idea. "Automated" equates to an electronically generated search for and extraction of facts facilitated by a pre-existing, third-party program, which is responding to a set of user-defined selection criteria.

On the other hand, a "manual" search engine is nothing more than a first-person extraction of facts. Touch a hot stove for the first time and information associating hot with pain is immediately registered. This is an excellent example of the migration of Absent Facts into the Universe of Present Facts through a result. A result occurs at the moment when there is an unambiguous migration of the undiscovered (absent) into the realm of the discovered (present). Think of the millions upon millions of facts that we accept as present which were, at one time in our lives, undiscovered. At the very beginning of development, at the beginning of the Cycle, we learn that hot will cause pain when touched; concrete is hard; you get hungry when you don't eat; etc. You get the idea.

Consider this staggering truth. About three generations ago, the manual search engine was how we all accessed the Universe of Present Facts. The automated search process did not yet exist. Before automation, our application of the manual search engine had a very specific term. It was called "living." The printed word, broadcasted mass media, family history from our elders, and yes, touching a hot stove, were all the manual selection processes that formed the data we extracted from the Universe of Present Facts. The extracted data was then processed through a set of tools used to transform the data into useful information. Those of you who have read Book 1 will relate when I refer to this form of useful information as a "Life Lesson."

The tools used to process data vary greatly from person to person and from culture to culture. Where there are countless tools available for use within the process of human development, with more being added every day, there are only two general categories: automated and manual. Yep, you are already ahead of me. This isn't rocket science. Automated tools are electronically based aids for the processing of extracted data, facilitated by a pre-existing, third-party program which is responding to a set of user-defined selection criteria. Thousands of automated data processing tools are at our command, with more being offered every day. Examples are everywhere: Excel, various apps on your smart phone, etc. Where would we be without the advances offered to humanity via the information and technology revolutions? Massive quantities of data can be processed instantly. The resulting output is limited only by the knowledge and imagination of the user. Today we hold in our hand (smart phones) many times the computing power that was used to put the first man on the moon. And the speed of the advancement, in the area of automated tools, is staggering. What a great time to be alive! "Alive," an interesting choice of words. This simple word carries significant implications as we explore how modern cultures learn and develop.

If access to these automated tools is so important in cultural development, surely everyone has equal access to these miracles of automation, correct? The answer, of course, is no. Variances in environmental and economic conditions (on the micro and macro levels) can drastically impact an individual's or culture's access to automated tools. These external influences may form insurmountable barriers, restricting a culture's access to mass quantities of data, thereby depriving one culture of information and knowledge which is held by another. These environmental and economic gaps existing between the "Haves" and "Have-nots" only widen as the technologies advance.

Think of it in terms of the Culture Model (Illustration #2). If one culture's environmental and economic conditions restrict its access to information and knowledge, compared to a culture with less restrictive access, would there not develop vast differences in the expectations held by the Haves versus those held by the Have-nots? Of course, there would be. These differences will result in an ever-widening communication gap based, at its core, on a lack of shared, common human experiences. Shared human experiences enable substantive communication between individuals and cultures forming the foundation of all productive relationships.

We know from our study of productive relationships that the absence of shared human experiences will foster an inability to

Shared experiences form the foundation of all productive relationships

anticipate the actions of another, creating a lack of trust between the cultures, which triggers an enhanced application of the relationship catalyst, which is emotion. The catalyst of purpose, which is integrity, will be called into doubt. When trust is lacking or integrity is called into question, a productive relationship depends on healing support from the foundation of substantive communication. The lack of shared human experiences hinders communication, slowing or stopping the healing process.

When a communication gap exists between the Haves and Have-nots, how would it be recognized? What would you look for in the day-to-day interactions between those with access to more information and knowledge, the Haves, and those whose access is more restricted, the Have-nots? First, one would see a growing intolerance of independent thought or non-conforming action. This intolerance would be directed inward at the individual members of the culture. The intolerances will be evident in both cultures, the Haves as well as the Have-nots. Within either culture, the root cause for intolerance would be founded upon a perceived lack of the basic human *need* of security. Please note that I used a qualifier, "perceived," when referring to the lack of security.

These created perceptions and the resulting restrictions are a direct result of the population granting influence to the leaders. The key influences granted by the population and exercised by cultural leaders are the shaping of future expectations, an external influence, and the selection of the substance contained within the communication, which is an internal influence. Please note that these key influences are both located at the bottom of the Cultural Model, making expectations and communication the foundational elements of culture. What other clear signs of a communication gap would be seen in the day-to-day interactions between the Haves and Have-nots?

One would see a rapid growth in aggressive behaviors directed outward toward the other culture. The Haves and the Have-nots would both aggressively react to the other's words and actions. Each would target the smallest deviation from their internal accepted cultural norms, labeling the other's deviation as the most abhorrent behavior imaginable. These ever-increasing reactions are directly related to the population granting influence to the leaders over the foundational elements of expectation and communication. The leaders, in turn, are using their influence to foster the perception of insecurity within the culture. On both sides of this relationship equation, you will see leaders create endless variations on the same themes: "How can you trust those other people? They are different from us. They think differently. They have access to different resources. Because they are different, they think they are better than we are. They want to destroy our way of life (our culture), which is an immediate threat to your future safety."

This silliness goes on every day, and with the proliferation of automated search engines and information tools, these ridiculous and harmful messages invade our lives twenty-four hours a day, seven days a week. WARNING: just because this method of influence sounds ridiculous, you would be mistaken to dismiss it. We are talking about influence, granted in good faith by the population, being used by leaders to instill fear within a culture. The constant and consistent application of fear is extremely effective when used to manipulate and restrict a culture. How do you know when cultures are being influenced by fear? Simple, cultures being influenced by fear will exhibit an increased use and acceptance of <u>ideology</u>. Ideology, when leveraged as influence over a culture, results in the population's acceptance of imposed expectations. For example, anyone identified by the cultural leader(s) who does not think, act, speak, or look like a member of our culture represents a dire threat to the population's safety.

I have just touched on several critical issues which go straight to the heart of the challenges faced by a leader wishing to transform a culture. Intolerance, in any form and regardless of its root cause, equates to cultural restriction. The counterbalance to intolerance, and one of the keys to successful cultural transformation, is <u>transparency</u>. The counterbalance to the use of ideology is a focus on actual <u>results</u>. To gain the benefit from actual results (shared experiences), the culture relies on transparency (the unrestricted access to information and knowledge). Keep these words in mind (choice, need, results, ideology, and transparency) when we move on to the next Life Questions. You will find these words and concepts to be critical in our exploration of truth, ideology, and ultimately, the Transformational Leadership Model. But for now, let's turn our attention back to learning the basic concepts surrounding

Ideology and intolerance equate to cultural restriction. A focus on transparency and results counterbalance these restrictions.

the Cycle and how it plays a significant role in the cultural development process. Understanding the Cycle puts our discussion of Haves, Have-nots, intolerance, and ideology into perspective.

We know that automated search engines and automated data processing tools share a set of common characteristics. Automated search engines and the related data processing tools are both electronically based aids for the processing of extracted data, facilitated by a pre-existing, third-party program, which is responding to a set of user-defined selection criteria.

It logically follows that manual search engines and manual data processing tools will also have common characteristics. Manual data processing tools are formed out of first-person experiences. Manual, when applied to the search engine process, equates to: I need to have personally read or witnessed the experience in order to select the required data. Manual, in the context of a data processing tool, has a slightly broader scope: I need to have personally read, witnessed, or anticipated the experience in order to more effectively process the extracted data into useable information. The addition of the human quality of anticipation to the scope of first-person opens the door for the uniquely human characteristics of expectation, curiosity, and yes, <u>faith</u> to enter into the cultural equation. Later, during our discussion of Life Question #3: "What is truth?" we take on the discussion of human faith. After reading that section, if I have chosen my words correctly, your perceptions surrounding faith may be expanded and hopefully, changed forever.

Progressing forward within the Cycle, the application of data processing tools, automated or manual, will generate variations within the information being created from the selected data. The application of each variation may then generate different results. In an unrestricted environment, these differing results will trigger the human *choice* of curiosity, causing the formation of an informational loop. Assuming that no outside influence restricts the choice of curiosity, the loop will return the learner to the Universe of Present Facts for a modified search. The modified search criteria may generate new, more accurate data which is then reprocessed by the tools to create another set of information to be used in the production of new results. Once the results are perceived as acceptable, the findings become part of the culture's knowledge.

On to the next level within the Cycle. Information evolves into knowledge. Knowledge resides within the population in the form of anticipated results which are frequently tested through multiple experiences. If the result of the repeated application of knowledge is constantly found to be as expected (each time we touch a hot stove, we experience pain), then the knowledge advances to the next level in the Cycle of Human Development and becomes an established skill. At this point, it is known that a hot stove, if touched, causes pain. The established knowledge and the developing skill can be expressed as follows: "Don't touch!"

What happens if we test our accepted knowledge and the experience does not conform to the anticipated result? We have now created a knowledge loop which, driven by the human *choice* for curiosity, forces the learner's return to the Universe of Present Facts and the human development process begins anew. Each curiosity loop, each informational iteration, leads us to new knowledge and new experiences. These opportunities to learn can be interrupted, restricting the culture's development, or they can be shared (transparency), serving to enhance/ strengthen the collective relationship.

Confirmation of knowledge, created through experiencing anticipated results, serves to develop skill. Humans develop skills through consistently experiencing the anticipated results from the application of knowledge. Developed skills must stand up to repeated application resulting in additional, anticipated experiences. Any unanticipated results from the application of acquired skills leads to yet another curiosity loop. However, at this level of human development, even the slightest deviation from the anticipated result is cause for curiosity. At the "skill" level of human development, there exists a near constant state of curiosity. Notice, in Illustration #3, the heavier lines, which denote a more frequently traveled path coming out from underneath the skill section and leading back to the Universe of Present Facts. It may seem to be counterintuitive to think that the further we progress along the Cycle, the more curious we become. Think of it logically. The more confident you are in anticipating a result, the more frequently you will apply the skill, which equates to your sense of surprise when unanticipated results emerge. Your being surprised by an unanticipated result generates an increased amount of energy which is directed toward curiosity. This newly formed sense of urgency (internal motivation) will send you back to the beginning of the Cycle in an attempt to better anticipate the result, honing our skills over and over again.

Let us continue our example of a hot stove being touched and resulting in pain. The toddler has developed the skills necessary to avoid touching the stove by making the assumption that it is always hot. What happens if the child, after attaining a developed level of skill, is confused when they see an adult touch the surface of the stove and not recoil in pain? At this point, the toddler's curiosity loop is quickly accessed and the development process is rapidly completed by using verbal communication (a manual tool) within an established, productive relationship (ask a parent). The child learns that the stove is not turned on; therefore, it is not hot. Witness the migration of absent facts into the present, resulting in a knowledge that the stove can exist in various states of hot ranging from cool to warm to hot. The possible range of actual results experienced by touching the stove now depends on newly acquired parameters: on; off; and the passage of time between the two.

Using this simplistic example, the child has attained the final stage of human development. They now understand the circumstances under which differing results can be anticipated. The application of understanding over multiple experiences, the results of which are accurately anticipated, provides the child with a modified purpose. Modified purpose is the final level of human development within the Cycle. He will be in a constant state of curiosity regarding his modified purpose (note the solid line back to the present facts). Is the stove turned off or on? How long ago was it last turned off or on? Are there visual signs regarding its temperature, etc.?

Here is an important fact to keep in mind. Attaining this new level of development is of no value to the culture, which in this case is the family, if the child chooses to withhold (restrict) this information. Not sharing the experience with his younger sister, who has not yet developed the knowledge or the skill to avoid the hot surface, restricts her development.

Stated in broader terms, individual progression within the Cycle is of no value to the culture if the experiences are not shared by and within the population. "How does a culture learn and develop?" We now know that one piece of the answer is: "By following the same development process as an individual." The key to cultural development, and therefore cultural transformation, is found in the sharing of experiences, or the substantive communication of expectations followed by actual results.

Shared experiences form the ability of a culture to establish common expectations, strengthened by substantive communication within and between cultures. Expectations and communication form the foundation on which all collective relationships are built. You want to know how to successfully lead cultural transformation? One part of the answer is to be transparent with the population regarding the actual results from the application of knowledge and skill. Take particular care when communicating the actual results. Be certain to share the results in a way that continuously improves the population's Universe of Present Facts, keeping the entire body of facts open for all to search, extract, and test. Transparency regarding results, both anticipated and actual, fuels curiosity and communication. This fuel keeps the Population's Growth Engine (PGE) engaged, enabling continued progression along the Cycle of Human Development.

Transparency regarding results, both anticipated and actual, fuels curiosity and communication.

As a leader, how can you better anticipate the results? One way of expressing this concept is: "A successful leader knows how to see around the corner." Remember when I stated earlier that I had invested the time necessary to learn about MB's culture so I could better anticipate the questions from the MB team? Allow me to address that question with a short story regarding my personal progression along the Cycle as I prepared for the MB transaction and cultural transformation.

There was a movie released in 1987 starring Michael J. Fox titled *The Secret of My Succe$s*. In this movie, Mr. Fox plays Brantley Foster, a young man trying to climb the ladder of success within the culture of big business (Corporate America). Through a series of unique circumstances, the character finds himself simultaneously serving in a dual role within the company (he was wearing multiple responsibility hats and was struggling to juggle the daily challenges—we can all relate).

The plot of the movie centers on the challenges of Brantley maintaining two roles, mailroom clerk and executive, without being discovered by the one person who knows his true identity, the CEO. Brantley is an entry-level employee in the mailroom, while simultaneously participating as the newest member of the company's executive leadership team.

In one scene, the CEO of the company, who only knows Brantley in his role as a clerk in the mailroom, enters the office of the newest member of his executive team. The CEO was trying to meet the allusive executive face to face for the first time. When the CEO pops in on the executive, hoping to catch him at his desk, he discovers Michael's character in the executive's office. The CEO makes the incorrect assumption that Brantley was there to deliver the mail.

The walls of the executive's office were completely covered with charts and graphs which were obviously produced by hand. There were stacks and stacks of computer printouts and corporate reports piled on the desk and the floor. As the CEO walks around the office, he asks the mailroom clerk if he had ever met this new exec. Brantley responds truthfully with "yes." Of course, he had met him; the two were one in the same.

The CEO continued his review of the material strewn about the office and then asked: "Where did he get all of this stuff?" The CEO was referring to the mountains of information about the company piled on the floor and mounted on the walls. Brantley slipped, just for an instant, out his mailroom clerk role and responded with: "This stuff is all available publicly through quarterly filings and the annual report." The CEO was clearly stunned by the answer but quickly returned to his self-absorbed world, dismissing the mail clerk and staying behind to pilfer through the assembled materials.

Okay, that is enough background from the movie to create the mental image. In the months leading up to my first meeting with the MB employees, my small, windowless office at RB's headquarters was very much like the office scene from the movie. I had spent hours combing through as much public information regarding MB as I could find. I researched MB's publicly available filings with the Securities and Exchange Commission (both quarterly and annual). I had piles of publicly available reports from multiple state and federal regulatory agencies. I had collected and researched every news article I could find on the company and their executive leadership team. I was able to attend a couple of after-hours business round tables where the MB CEO and CFO were keynote speakers. I monitored daily the trading volume and price of MB's stock. I was immersed in reports and projections from market analysts reviewing and projecting MB's performance. There were maps showing existing RB offices and the overlapping locations of MB. I studied MB's regional and national competitors. The desk, floor, and walls of my office were covered with charts, graphs, and reports related to MB.

Let's review. I had used both automated and manual search engines and informational tools to extract data from my rapidly expanding Universe of Present Facts regarding MB. Next, as I progressed down the Cycle, the information I was generating regarding MB was tested against MB's actual results, the opinions of analysts following the company, the actions of competitors, and my own experiences in the financial services industry. Each time a result was discovered that did not match the anticipated result, my curiosity led me to return to the beginning of the Cycle and a renewed selection process. After a significant investment of time, my knowledge began to increase regarding the strategic direction, financial priorities, and cultural structure of MB. The anticipated results, which were based on my MB knowledge, helped me to form the pricing model and benefit profiles (benefit profiles for both RB and MB) for the proposed transaction. Through the sharing of this knowledge, my team and I developed the strategic, operational objectives (establishing a set of expectations) for the post-conversion market.

When I walked in front of the MB team for the first time, how could I have been in a position to "see around the corner" and anticipate their questions? Weeks and weeks of transaction-specific work, combined with years of leadership experience, helped develop my understanding of the transaction from RB's perspective and MB's perspective, both cultural and strategic. This is how I was able to anticipate the circumstances related to this transaction from RB's and MB's points of view. I understood the financial, cultural, and strategic *choices* and *needs* of both sides, and I was able to anticipate the resulting influences.

This level of knowledge, which evolved into skill, enabled me to be prepared and enabled me to better prepare my team for that first meeting. I understood the *choices* and *needs* of the individuals in front of me. I understood well the expectations of the groups I represented through my Core of Responsibility (RB's customers, shareholders, and culture).

My understanding of the Cycle, basic human *choices* and *needs*, and my Core of Responsibility provided me with the courage required to step to the front, raise my hand, and tell the assembled group that I was the person they should hold accountable for their new circumstances. It was the moment that I was granted influence over the new RB employees' cultural transformation. My Core and my team knew that I was accountable for anything that went wrong. They also knew that I had pledged to give them the credit for any and all successes. And now, I had set that same expectation for the MB employees. Was I crazy? No. I had confidence in my knowledge, my team, and the Core that stood behind me. Was it a risk? Huge. Did we meet our goals? Oh, my goodness, yes. I would not recommend that you go around raising your hand and assuming responsibility for the mistakes of others, at least not yet. We still have some information to gather and knowledge to test before I would recommend taking that particular leap of faith.

Understanding the Cycle is just one part of the leadership skill set needed to see around the corner and own the future. The next skill needed to improve your odds of correctly anticipating the future frames the second part of our answer to the question: "How do cultures learn and develop?" It is time for us to explore human *choices* and *needs*.

Cultural Learning and Development: Choices and Needs

Let's begin by understanding how and why human *choices* and *needs* impact cultural learning and development. The best place to start is by sharing my own personal *choices* and *needs*. During our exploration of human *choices* and *needs,* we will discover that, as with the Cycle, a leader's *choices* and *needs* correlate closely with those of the culture. Why? Answer: the personal *choices* and *needs* of the leader will have a profound influence over the population being led. Let's look at *choices* and *needs* in more manageable pieces. First, my *choices*.

My personal *choices* for growth (humility, curiosity, courage, and integrity) were part of who I was long before my meeting with the MB team. These *choices*, which I make anew on a daily basis, were part of who I was thirty plus years ago and remain an important part of who I am today.

Humility resulted from lessons learned at the age of eighteen during my first semester in college when I experienced firsthand, individuals with God-given gifts of talent, both intellectual and athletic. These life-altering experiences helped to start me out on a journey which led me to discover and develop my own talents. Ultimately, these early experiences helped me to learn how to discover and develop the hidden talents within each individual around me.

Curiosity has been a constant companion of mine. I have always chosen to explore not only the "how" but also to dig deep and discover the "why." How things worked held my interest even at a young age, but understanding "why" they worked the way they did was the driving force that kept and keeps me learning.

Courage, in particular the *choice* of Quiet Courage, has been paired with my *choice* of humility ever since I decided that I was going to succeed in life, regardless of my dad's frequently expressed opinions to the contrary. Many times during my leadership career, the application of Quiet Courage has enabled me to succeed, to discover opportunity where others had failed.

And finally, there is *integrity,* the strength of will to do the right thing even when no one is watching. Again, this was a choice I made in my formative years when facing difficult personal circumstances. My *choice* of integrity is reflected in Leadership Rule #1: "Always be professional, which begins with respect for yourself and everyone around you." Integrity is simply a *choice* to always show respect to everyone, including yourself.

> *Integrity is simply a choice to always show respect to everyone, including yourself.*

My growth, your growth, and all human growth is a function of the *choices* we make and the *needs* we all strive to satisfy. Our *needs* work together with our *choices* to form the Personal Growth Engine, or the Population Growth Engine, both of which are expressed by the same acronym PGE. (Much more regarding PGE can be found in Book 1.) Just as there are four basic *choices* that all humans make, there are four levels of *need* that we all share. These human *needs* are safety, security, purpose, and love.

Growth through the process of human *choice* is the result of a series of independent decisions made daily. In fact, growth through *choice* is the cumulative effect of the decisions we make every minute of every day. Today I may decide to be curious, but tomorrow I may change my mind and decide to accept things as they are. My decisions between curiosity and complacency can be changed at will and made independently from the other three *choices.*

On the other hand, growth through the satisfaction of human *need* is an interdependent progression. For example, if my *need* for safety is not met, and I am in fear for my day-to-day survival, 100 percent of my resources will be focused to ensure my immediate safety. There will be no time for and no thought given to any other need, other than "survive for another day."

The next level of *need*, security, can only be attained when I perceive that the circumstances providing for my safety will remain in place for the foreseeable future. My ability to anticipate future security is completely dependent upon my continued perception of safety.

Reaching the third level of *need,* purpose, is actually a reward for improving the human condition. The opportunity to satisfy the *need* for purpose is a luxury which can only be attained after one perceives themselves as secure. Purpose, defined as what you wish to accomplish through your future growth, is the reward that one earns after first achieving safety, then securing it for the foreseeable future. This is why we state that human *needs* are an interdependent progression, one building on the other, and not a moment to moment decision, as is the case with *choice*.

Ultimately, once the human growth process satisfies the *need* for purpose, the leader is free to develop the final level of *need*, love. Love, the verb, is achieved when the leader realizes the *need* to extend themselves for the benefit of others by identifying and meeting their <u>legitimate</u> *needs* (safety, security, and purpose) and seeking <u>their</u> greatest good. Please note that the leader is seeking the greatest good for the person(s) they are leading, not their own. Also note that the leader's objective is to meet the "legitimate" *needs* of others. The goal is not to fulfill a wish list of wants.

The human *need* for love, the verb, is met when the growth process has achieved a level where the leader's purpose is solidly established and well-defined. Love is attained when the leader is ready to extend, or to risk themselves for the benefit of another individual or group. The willingness to risk oneself for the benefit of others is not designed to provide for their wants (their wish list). Rather love is the *need* to help others earn the luxury of purpose in the hope that they, too, will someday grow to achieve the *need* to love. To put the *need* for love simply, an individual's purpose evolves to a level where they *need* to give of themselves solely for the benefit of others.

Now that we have a snapshot of the growth process, PGE, we need to return to Life Question #2: "How do cultures learn and develop?"

Answer: In exactly the same manner as the individual(s) who lead them. Recall that the "P" in PGE stands for either "Personal" or "Population." PGE processes are dependent upon the leader's progression along the Cycle of Human Development combined with the *choices* the leader makes and level of *need* the leader has achieved.

Leadership, the ability to influence the lives (the futures) of those around us, is as important of a responsibility as there is. That is the "why" behind these books. My hope is to influence and to help others that have been called to lead, by helping them to first understand the process of leadership and then enabling them to effectively teach the next generation of leaders. The effective influence of a culture begins when you have confidence in your own *choices* and *needs,* and you understand well the *choices* and *needs* of the populations you represent.

Human *choices* and *needs*, combined with progression along the Cycle of Human Development, are two of the sources which generate external cultural influences (environmental, economic, and expectations) and internal cultural influences (trust, integrity, and communication). Together, these influences form the Culture Model (shown in Illustration #2). We now have two (the Cycle plus *choices* and *needs*) of the three parts of the answer to: "How do cultures learn and develop?" The Core of Responsibility is the missing piece in our understanding of cultural learning and development. But, before we move on to the third and final part of our answer, allow me to share a short life lesson that will demonstrate the power of *choice* and *need*.

This particular life lesson is one of my favorites because it is an extremely flexible illustration. I have used this story countless times to teach leaders negotiation skills. It has been used to teach the critical nature of timing in the leadership process. I have also used it to illustrate our current topic, the power of *choice* and *need* within the influence (leadership) process. There are so many opportunities to learn buried within this story. I hope it speaks to you as it has to so many others.

The meeting with the MB team took place in late spring and this life lesson took place in the early fall of that same year. When you are seeking to strategically grow an organization through the process of mergers and acquisitions (M&A), you always have two or three deals in the works at the same time. This particular opportunity was one that was in the hopper, but not one that I had personally developed. It actually had been provided to me through an outside legal firm that RB had engaged for an earlier acquisition.

Before we get to the actual event, here is a brief summary of the back-story. A small savings and loan in northeastern Kentucky had converted to a stock corporation a couple of years earlier and was now in search of a bigger company to purchase them. Their legal firm had a working relationship with the legal firm we had used for a previous deal. When one of my contacts at the firm learned of the potential deal, they picked up the phone and called me to see if I had any interest. Northeastern Kentucky was a stretch for RB, but it was part of our three-year strategic plan, just a couple years early in the process. But when opportunity knocks, you at least need to peek outside to see what is there.

The more I looked at the deal, the more interesting it appeared to be. After some market research, operations modeling, and discussions with our board of directors, it was decided to pursue the acquisition. Preliminary discussions proceeded quickly, and we reached the point where it was time for RB to sit down face to face with the savings bank's (RB-KY) legal team. Time for us to negotiate!

Up to this point, all of the conversations with their attorney had taken place through our legal firm, so this meeting would be the first time for the two sides to actually meet. The date was set and RB's negotiation team was selected. On our side of the table would be RB's CEO, CFO, and me. Representing the savings bank at the negotiating table would be their legal team made up of three attorneys from RB-KY's firm. The day arrived and off to the airport I went to meet their legal team.

It was a beautiful fall day. Calm winds with blue skies and just enough chill were in the air to let you know that winter was on its way. The airport they were flying into was a small, regional airport located about twenty minutes from RB's headquarters. I knew the airport well. At the time, there was a shuttle service that connected with a national hub in Pittsburgh, PA. In my previous job with a Fortune 500 corporation, I used this path to the Pittsburgh hub many times as I made my way to and from corporate headquarters in Houston, TX.

But today's trip was way more interesting to me. This opportunity with the northeastern Kentucky corporation had become of personal interest. If successful in the acquisition, it was possible that I would be promoted to president and CEO of a newly formed RB subsidiary. Only time would tell.

I pulled up to the parking area in my white Chevy Suburban, hopped out, and went inside the terminal to wait on their flight to arrive. At the appointed time, I went to stand at the windows overlooking the runway to watch their flight land. To my surprise, appearing on the horizon was a small private (or chartered) jet. The jet gracefully touched down and taxied to the unloading area. I grabbed a pull cart and headed to the plane to see if I could help them with their luggage.

The door on their plane dropped open. The first two men emerging from the jet were cookie-cutter, young, urban professionals. Both were in their late twenties. They were impeccably dressed, carrying obviously new and expensive leather luggage. These guys looked like they were stepping off the pages of a magazine. I greeted them with: "Hi. I'm Rob. Can I help you with your bags?" These first two gentlemen shook my hand, grunted a greeting, and handed me their luggage. "How was your flight?" I asked. "Well, we made it!" was one reply, followed by the second gentleman chiming in: "Ya… barely. Do you know we had to circle the airport twice while they cleared deer off the runway?!" At that moment, I knew I was going to have fun with these two. They were obviously full of themselves and were going to be aggressive at the negotiation table. I loved getting these personality types at the table. There was money to be made for the RB shareholders when I was fortunate enough to get an arrogant, aggressive person on the other side.

I suspected that these first two attorneys were just along for the experience. After I placed their luggage on the cart, I looked up, and emerging from the plane was a third gentleman. He was slight in build, and I judged him to be just a little older than I was, maybe in his late-thirties. His luggage was also leather but well-worn and frayed. He smiled the moment he stepped off the plane, reached for my hand, introduced himself, and immediately thanked me for picking them up. When I asked him if I could take his luggage, he replied: "No thank you. I've got it." When I asked him about his flight, his response was noticeably different from the first two: "Great! This is a lovely part of the country, and what a beautiful day." Yep, this was the guy I needed to pay attention to. He clearly was the lead negotiator.

His demeanor was one of confidence, while being polite, unassuming, and sincere. This gentleman could have just flown through a hurricane and you would never know it. To the outside world, every flight this guy takes is great. He was quick with a smile, and you could bet that he was always in control of his emotions. The two youngsters were going to be constantly nipping at my heels, but this third guy was clearly capable of handing me my head at the negotiating table and smiling the entire time he was doing it. Hot dog, what a great chance for me to learn!

The twenty-minute ride to the hotel was more of the same. The two junior attorneys commented from the back seat on how rural the area was, while the lead attorney sat quietly in the front passenger seat. The only time he spoke was to ask me how long a drive I had to get to the office each morning and if I had a family.

The hotel where they were staying was a part of the area's rich history. Recently remodeled, I knew from experience that the hotel's rooms were very comfortable and their food was excellent. Our guests should have a very enjoyable stay for the one night they would be with us. I unloaded the truck and carried the bags into the lobby for the two gentlemen. The other gentleman insisted on carrying his own luggage. Once they were checked in, I asked if I could be of any further service. The answer was a dismissive "no." Before I left, we arranged for me to pick them up in the hotel lobby around 8:30 the next morning. I had about a thirty-minute drive home. During my trip home that evening,

I used what I had just learned to develop a series of anticipated results from tomorrow's meeting.

The next morning, I arrived at the hotel a little before 8:30. All three gentlemen were in the lobby and ready to get the day started. I, of course, asked about their stay at the hotel. I received two responses that consisted of grumblings about the room and the food. The third response was cheerful and clear: "Great! How was your evening?" You know who made which comment. I couldn't wait to get to the table. This day was going to be fun!

It was only a couple minutes from the hotel to RB's headquarters. RB had beautiful facilities. Originally built in 1902 and recently remodeled and expanded, our buildings, offices, and technology were all points of pride for our company. I gave them a quick tour, ending up at the board room, where we had coffee, juice, and a light breakfast waiting. After making the introductions, I asked if I could get anyone anything. The two youngsters and the RB CFO asked me to bring them some coffee, which I was more than happy to do. Our CEO, the lead attorney, and I helped ourselves. After the obligatory exchange of pleasantries, we got down to the business at hand.

The morning went as anticipated. The youngsters attacked everything from the assumptions built into the pricing model to the language contained within the draft of the Purchase and Assumptions Agreement. As the two attacked, our CFO was more than anxious to take the bait, counterattacking at every opportunity. He inserted himself into the process with very little knowledge of the deal's structure, and aggressively argued, on RB's behalf, regarding multiple points of contention. The lead attorney, RB's CEO, and I sat quietly as this back-and-forth escalated. Finally, RB's CEO called for a short break. I immediately got up and began clearing the trash off the table and asked if I could get something for anyone else. The orders came my way asking for coffee, juice, pastries, and fruit, which I was happy to bring to the table.

The meeting had a hard stop scheduled for early afternoon because our CEO had previous obligations. So, when we resumed our second round of discussions, it was clear that we had not made much progress and time for meaningful discussion was growing short. The back-and-forth picked up right where it had left off; the youngsters would start yapping and our CFO would yap back. This foolishness continued until our CFO had reached his breaking point. With nothing having been resolved and after a particularly heated exchange, our CFO stood up from the table and left the room. He did not return. After his exodus from the room, the youngsters declared the negotiating session to be a waste of their time and began to pack up their papers. The CEO called for another short break. I gathered the trash off the table and delivered coffee and juice.

What I wanted to see happen during this strategic break was a private meeting between the lead attorney and our CEO. Sure enough, they each fixed themselves a cup of coffee and stood by the food table in quiet conversation. Shortly after this private meeting began, the CEO motioned me over and invited me to join in. A couple minutes after I joined the conversation, the lead attorney excused himself, leaving the CEO and me to discuss our options for where we would go from there. While he and I spoke, the lead attorney returned to the table and huddled with the other two. At this point in the morning, it was about an hour before lunch would be brought in.

When we returned to the table, the CEO spent most of our remaining time laying out the numerous advantages to RB-KY's shareholders by holding RB's stock. He talked about his vision for the future and how the Kentucky acquisition would be incorporated into RB's operations. These topics were his strongest areas. He excelled at articulating a clear vision of the future, a vision filled with purpose and ripe with expectations. He knew our results by heart and created a compelling picture as to why their culture would be a great fit with our culture.

As the meeting came to a close, I gathered the trash from the table as the attorneys shook hands with the CEO and thanked him for his time. The four of us climbed back into my Suburban and began the short trip back to the airport. I don't recall what, if anything, was said during the twenty-minute ride. When we reached the terminal, the youngsters hopped out, grabbed their luggage, and headed at a brisk pace to board the waiting plane. The lead attorney and I walked together, more slowly, making our way to the terminal. When we entered the building, he asked me to watch his luggage while he stepped into the men's room before boarding the little jet.

In a couple minutes he returned, and we shook hands before he turned to walk outside and get on the plane. I will never forget what happened next. After taking about three steps toward the door, he stopped and turned around. He walked back to where I was standing and with a sheepish grin across his face, he said: "Rob, what do you need?" I didn't even bother to pretend that I didn't understand what he was asking. At that moment, I knew he had figured it out. He had reached the conclusion that I was actually the decision maker in this deal. It was clear that, while sitting silently at the table, he had spent his day assembling the pieces of the puzzle (returning over and over again to search his expanding Universe of Present Facts), looking for additional opportunities for his client (testing his knowledge and observing the results). At some point during the day, he had reached a level of comfort in his knowledge, supported by the skills that he had developed through experience, which led him to his conclusion. He knew that I, the guy who carried the luggage, fetched coffee, and cleared the trash, was actually the guy who held the influence over this transaction.

Notice that after he assembled the pieces and chose to ask the question, he chose his words very carefully. His question was: "What do you need?" and not the more typical question: "What do you want?" His selection of words indicated that he anticipated me to be at a level of development that would enable him to skip the normal steps of positioning and posturing. He concluded that we could go straight to the heart of the deal, the *need* of purpose. Through his choice of words, he was basically telling me: "Look, I have wasted my morning and the jet is waiting. What will it take to get this deal done for my clients? What do you need in order to accomplish your purpose for this transaction? Here is what my client needs…"

He and I stood in the lobby of the terminal and over the next fifteen minutes, we agreed on the basic structure of a deal which was successfully completed about four months later. The private plane waited patiently on the tarmac as we talked. However, his two traveling partners weren't as patient as the pilot. I was facing the plane as we spoke, so I could see them appear in the jet's door, stare into the terminal attempting to catch a glimpse of what was going on, and then disappear back into the plane. "Thanks Rob. Good doing business with you. I will be in touch next week after I have spoken with my clients, and we can get started on the details. Beautiful part of the country!" And with that being said, he shook my hand, slung his suit bag over his shoulder, and boarded the plane back to Washington, DC.

There are so many life lessons to be illustrated from this single event. But, before I summarize the takeaways, allow me to turn the clock forward and close the loop for you. As I mentioned earlier, the transaction was completed about four months later. The lead attorney was good to his word regarding the *needs* of his clients, and I held to my word regarding RB's list of *needs*. There were no surprises, which is unusual in a transaction of this complexity. Jennifer, Adam, and I did relocate to northeastern Kentucky. I became CEO of the new company but, more importantly, Jennifer and I found our forever home.

About ten months after RB acquired RB-KY, the same attorney and I were engaged in negotiations over a second acquisition. It was also located in the northeastern Kentucky market. This time, he and I handled the particulars of the transaction over the phone, avoiding a repeat of the drama in the board room. The second acquisition had a couple of challenges, but nothing that he and I couldn't work through.

I learned shortly after our time at the airport that this gentleman was one of the nation's leading M&A attorneys for this segment of business. I knew he was good; I just didn't know how good. He specialized in converting mutually owned savings and loans and tightly held small banks into publicly traded stock companies. Then, at the appropriate time, he guided them through the selling process. This gentleman made a very good living by being one of the best in his field. He was a tireless worker with a no-nonsense reputation, possessing a high level of skill and integrity. Oh, by the way, the two junior attorneys, the youngsters as I called them earlier, were along for the experience, as expected. If I recall correctly, both were Ivy League grads and brilliant attorneys. They were there to play a role (aggressive, always on the attack) in order to learn how to anticipate the behavior of others when they are placed under pressure at the negotiating table. This was all part of their professional Cycle: information, knowledge, skill, and finally, understanding. It is amazing the number of opportunities life grants you for learning, if you only know how to recognize them. So, what are our primary takeaways from this event? Here are three, of several, written in no particular order.

First, in cultural development, as well as productive relationship management, things are rarely as they initially appear. The learning loops built within the Cycle represent the pathways to learning (perceiving) the facts about people and circumstances. Interrupting the Cycle's learning loop by choosing not to be curious will deny you the opportunity of learning (seeing) how things truly are.

> *Being "right" in anticipating a result is an opportunity for you to teach others by setting the example. Being "wrong" about an anticipated result is an opportunity for you to learn.*

Next, anticipating results and then experiencing the actual outcomes is by far the most effective and efficient way that humans (individually or culturally) learn. The lack of transparency, hiding, or modifying the results restricts the migration of Absent Facts into the Universe of Present Facts. This restriction limits our ability to accurately anticipate results, which leads to a heightened state of insecurity. A reduced sense of the *need* of security impedes the natural progression to the *need* of purpose. A lack of security impedes purpose, restricts knowledge, and curtails the *choice* of curiosity. If you don't know what to expect, how can you learn from the actual results? Simple. Being "right" in anticipating a result is an opportunity for you to teach others by setting the example. Being "wrong" about an anticipated result is an opportunity for you to learn. By adopting this simple perception of risk, there is benefit, regardless of the outcome. Have the courage to stay curious. You win either way.

Third, development along the Cycle, the progression of human *need,* and establishing a foundation for *choice* are all dependent on an acquired sense of right and wrong. We will learn during our exploration of "truth," that much of who we are, individually and culturally, is dependent on the influences from our perceived Core of Responsibility. The Core is the last part of the answer to Life Question #2: "How do cultures learn and develop?"

Cultural Learning and Development: The Core of Responsibility

The Core of Responsibility (the "Core") represents our collective or individual reference point from which we perceive ourselves and the world around us. It is our chosen perspective. Readers of Book 1 (<u>LIVE better LEAD differently</u>) will understand this statement: Our Core is a reflection of our answers to the all-important relationship question: "What is in it for me?" How we collectively (culturally) or individually define "me" and how we prioritize those answers is a direct result of our Core perspectives. Just as a quick review, your definition of "me" may be: my country, my family, or my faith. Another set of definitions may be: my company, my customers, or my community. Experience has taught me that others rarely defined "me" as "myself."

Notice that the perspectives generated by the Core result in *choices* and reflect *needs.* We know, from the previous section, that human *choices* and *needs* have a profound influence on the progression of development within the Cycle. For example, when the Core focuses on me, defined as myself, it is most likely true that the individual or culture making that *choice* has not progressed beyond the *need* of security. As a result, their future development will be restricted. Do you see how these three concepts (the Cycle, human *choices* and *needs*, and the Core) all work in concert to enhance, or restrict, individual and cultural learning and development? Good. You are making excellent progress. Let's keep moving forward.

You may be surprised to know that the Core of Responsibility Model was actually created prior to the Relationship Model. "How" it was first developed, and more importantly "why" it was created is an interesting story and may help with understanding the Core's application within both the leadership and cultural transformation processes. We begin with understanding the "why."

Perspectives generated by the Core result in choices and reflect needs.

As is true with almost all of the illustrations and concepts presented in this series of books, the motivation behind the creative process was the need for me to find a way to present an intangible concept, making it appear tangible to an audience of leaders. The teaching method of associating the intangible to the tangible enhances the transferability of any concept (witness the association of a car engine to the Personal/Population Growth Engine). Enhanced transferability facilitates an effective and efficient communication process, building confidence in the data being delivered, which in turn promotes progression along the Cycle. You get the idea. Making concepts come alive for the audience helps them to learn better and faster.

I had been working in the health care industry for about three years. Learning an entirely new business model (a community controlled and not-for-profit medical system vs. a publicly traded very much for profit corporation). During this time, I had developed a solid understanding of the organization's culture. Just as a quick note, this is the same medical system that I used to frame the "Transitional Conversation" at the beginning of Book 1. In short, the medical system was around 4,500 employees at the time and was the region's largest employer.

During my tenure, I had been assigned ever-increasing leadership responsibilities, which had recently elevated me to one of the medical system's senior administrators. Up to this point, most of my responsibilities had revolved around the organization's business operations and financial systems. However, a series of events, the details of which will be the subject of Book 3's

Associating the intangible to the tangible enhances the transferability of any concept

opening conversation, had placed me in the position of leading the processes of change and cultural transformation within the medical system. My willingness to accept this new leadership role required me by strategic design and cultural necessity to become a Transformational Leader. Also, by strategic design and after about eighteen months, my Transformational Leadership role would, out of necessity, evolve into a Terminal Leadership role.

For those of you familiar with leading purposeful change and cultural transformation, you know what I am talking about. As you become the leader of transformation, you must become a catalyst for change. "Catalysts" are typically consumed during the process of change, or they are removed at some point during the transformational reaction. In either case, as a catalyst for change, my days with the organization were numbered. Best case, I had about twenty-four months to effect the transformation before I would either step aside or be removed.

It was at the beginning of that twenty-four-month period that I found myself in need of a way to transfer to other leaders the intangible concepts which make up the Core of Responsibility. Up to this point, the instructional tools I had developed to teach change management and cultural transformation had mostly centered around the use of illustrations based on two axis, x and y. I had used these visuals for years, expressing the critical concepts of change in terms of "Results Over Time." In addition to Results Over Time, I would frequently use illustrations based on an equilateral triangle, but they were static models. One example was the use of the triangle to communicate Maslow's Hierarchy of Needs. (In 1943, psychologist Abraham Maslow stated that people are motivated to achieve certain needs, and that some needs take precedence over others.) I also used it to illustrate the concept of organizational structure, using the standard equilateral triangle to represent several variations on the traditional Top-Down Organizational Structure and my favorite, the inverted triangle, representing an organizational structure where those closest to the point of service are given the highest priority. In each of these three cases, my use of the equilateral triangle was static, meaning the illustration was not designed to change as circumstances changed. My use of static modeling would not help the audience learn to anticipate the effect of future results.

I needed to create an illustration which would allow me to transfer to the audience of leaders the intangible concept of three interacting variables, not just a historic look at two variables (Results Over Time). The new illustration would also need to be dynamic, allowing us to learn by modeling anticipated results and showing their expected impact on the Core. But, all I had was a blank page staring back at me. The blank legal pad was on my lap. The pencil was in my hand, and the airplane was pulling back from the gate.

This was the first time I had been on an airplane in about fifteen years. And, FYI, I haven't taken another flight since then, which was about twelve years ago. Please understand, I have no fear of flying. In fact, I enjoy the feeling of acceleration during takeoff and like everyone else, rejoice after a smooth landing. No, it is the process of flying that I despise. To those of you whose daily schedules are subject to the forces of nature and the follies of man, I salute you! You have my respect and my sympathy. To those who work daily in the organized chaos, which is the air transportation system, you also have my respect and my undying gratitude. How you do as well as you do, given the circumstances you are faced with every day, is a wonder. Thank you for keeping us safe!

For me, avoiding air travel is a *choice* which I can make because I have earned the luxury of purpose. I wouldn't invest the time to walk across the street, much less fly, for the purposes of self-promotion. I will, however, drive for hours, or yes, even get on an airplane if my purpose is to help others learn or to learn more myself.

Twelve years ago, that was indeed the purpose underlying my choosing to travel beyond a reasonable driving distance. The flight's destination presented me with both an opportunity to teach and to learn. The anticipated result was that, after this trip, I would be better able to help my Core in the transformation process. The purpose was to discover new information and knowledge for the benefit of my Core. In order to do so, and in keeping with the Cycle, I needed to expand my Universe of Present Facts. If successful, I would return home with the ability to better help other leaders anticipate future results related to the massive software conversion and automation upgrade the medical system was about to undertake. No process, no department, and no team member within the medical system would be untouched by this software conversion. The Core's need for a successful transformation was great.

The page was still blank as the jet paused as it approached the start of the runway and the pilot engaged the engines. I took a moment to enjoy the feeling of acceleration during takeoff. Seated next to me and serving as my all-important guide to successfully navigating my first post-9/11 flight was Sarah, who has given me permission to use her real name. Even at a young age, Sarah was a very talented Subject Matter Expert. Her skill for understanding and explaining complex systems and processes rivaled those of Jill, from my earlier years with RB. Both ladies had God-given intellectual talents and a natural ability to lead. While my path with Jill was cut short because of my changing circumstances after the RB-KY deal, my leadership path with Sarah had only recently begun.

Sarah was and is an aggressive learner. She is fearless in her acceptance of challenge and change. Sarah has the ability to tolerate way more personal risk than most leaders would ever accept. This unique ability is a function of courage formed out of her own life experiences, which I will leave to her to share with the world, or not, through the writing of her own book.

One more point regarding Sarah, then we will get back to filling the blank page. She and I would work together at the medical system for another couple of years beyond the date of this flight, but even after our paths separated, we have stayed in touch. She went on to realize incredible growth as a leader. Sarah is currently a senior level leader in one of the nation's fastest growing health care companies. The accomplishments she could list on a resume are truly impressive, but her personal growth dwarfs any job-related honor. The work to get where she is today was hers. The sacrifices were hers, and the accomplishments are hers and hers alone. My role was to facilitate Sarah's leadership growth by helping her to change her perception of others, enabling her to benefit from viewing people and processes using different perspectives. The blank page in front of me, and my need to develop a dynamic method for illustrating the Core's concepts, proved to be an excellent opportunity for both of us to learn and to teach.

The creative process began with listing three critical groups on the blank page. First on the list was "*Customer,*" which we defined as all of the medical system's in-patients, out-patients, admitting physicians, vendors, and professional service providers. It is an all-inclusive list. Second was "shareholder," which evolved because of the medical system's legal structure to "stakeholder" and finally to "community." (For the purposes of this book, let's stick with the original term of *shareholder.*) The third critical group listed was initially written as "team members" but evolved into the more appropriate label of *"Culture."* With the three critical groups labeled and defined, we now had what would become the Core of Responsibility Model. The question remained: "What could we use as a visual that would enable us to make the intangible appear tangible? What visual could we use to illustrate three equally important groups? Changes impacting three equally important groups... Delta! That was the answer. The fourth letter of the Greek alphabet, Delta, is written in the form of an equilateral triangle with three equal sides representing three equal groups. That works. There was another factor that made the use of Delta the perfect choice. The factor was a personal context that gave Delta a special meaning to me.

Before joining the medical system, I was part of the leadership team that helped build, and eventually sell, a small regional savings and loan. One of the members of the board of directors was an accomplished businessman and an engineer by training and profession. Just about every board meeting, I could count on him to ask me: "What is the Delta on that?" His meaning was to quantify and explain the change in the number, or concept, being presented. What caused that result? The shape and the personal context made Delta the right answer.

Constructing the visual aid by first drawing the three-sided symbol for change was the perfect way to connect with my audience. After all, my accepted purpose was to facilitate and to help leaders better understand the process and cultural change. I added the equilateral triangle to the page. We now had the list of three variables paired with our three-sided visual. The next task was to assemble the model.

Customer was assigned to the left side of Delta. The interests of the customer are counterbalanced against the interests of the shareholder, so the right side was labeled as shareholder. The next step was easy and made perfect sense. Culture's place was clearly at the base of the triangle, supporting the interests of both the customer and the shareholder. See Illustration #4: The Core of Responsibility below.

The visual aid being complete, we turned our attention to the presentation aspects of the model. How do you meaningfully explain the dynamic relationship between leadership and the three Core groups? The eventual answer was: Express the relationship between the three Core groups in the form of results. Results are something to which all leaders can relate. Results are tangible and quantifiable. But which results? There are thousands from which to choose, correct? Historic? Current? Future? Yes, to all three questions. Historic and current results are included for

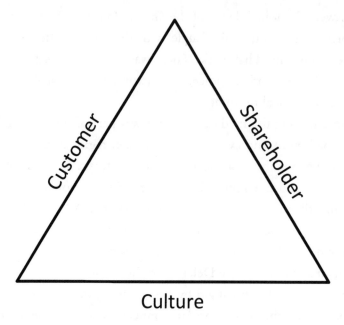

the benefit of context and the anticipated future results frame the purpose (the objective) of change. Within these three sets of results, there are an infinite number of variables to consider, but there are only two result categories which capture the purpose of the Core groups: *Quality* in all of its forms and functions and *Finance*, again in all of its forms.

> *Result is critical to the leadership process because it provides the needed vehicle for communicating the dynamics of change.*

Now we had the missing fourth element, "Result." Result is critical to the leadership process because it provides the needed vehicle for communicating the dynamics of change. It deserved inclusion into the developing model, and it needed to be prominently displayed to reflect its importance. The challenge was the introduction of a fourth variable into a three-sided visual. The solution was both simple and visually effective. It was the use of a teeter-totter.

Resting atop of the equilateral triangle would be a single line repre-senting *Results*. The line would be intersected at its midpoint (like the fulcrum of a teeter-totter), representing the daily challenge to all leaders maintaining a reasonable balance between the customer's need for (per-ception of) *Quality* goods and services versus the shareholder's need for (perception of) an acceptable *Financial* return on their investment. See Illustration #5: The Balanced Growth Model below.

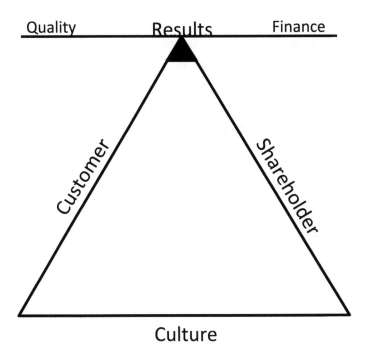

Once the new model was sketched out on the paper, we began test-ing its functionality by altering customer and shareholder perceptions. If the customer group perceived the need for improved Quality, then the Quality side of the Results line would be weighted more heavily, moving it closer to the customer's side of the model. When the focus of the Culture is placed on Quality (meeting the needs of the customer base), there is less of a priority placed on Financial results. This moves the Finance side of the Results line farther away from the shareholder group.

Based on this configuration, leadership can anticipate future Quality results to improve, while Financial results will be less favorable.

Continuing our test of the model, if the shareholder group perceived the need for improved financial performance, then the Finance side of the Results line would be weighted more heavily, moving it closer to the shareholder's side of the model. When the focus of the Culture is placed on financial performance (meeting the needs of the shareholder group), there is less of a priority placed on Quality. This moves the Quality side of the Results line farther away from the Customer base. Based on this configuration, leadership can anticipate future Financial results to improve, while Quality results will be less favorable.

To state all this in a different way, this was a great way of transferring the "how" and the "why" behind the old Cost vs. Benefit model to an audience of leaders. The dynamics of the new model would enable me to effectively illustrate the leadership challenges created for the Culture by changes in the perceptions of the customer base and/or shareholder group. Balanced Results can only be maintained through Cultural transformation in response to shifting perceptions. The model worked!

> *Quality and Finance are balanced on the point of perception formed by the customer and the shareholder and supported by a strong Culture.*

Now, we needed a summary statement, a simple statement that would connect the leader to the model, making it memorable and real. After several drafts, we hit on the summary statement: "Quality and Finance are balanced on the point of perception formed by the customer and the shareholder and supported by a strong Culture." That was the tag line and, over time, it proved to be very effective.

But the model wasn't complete, because it was void in the middle. We needed to illustrate the support structure within the Balanced Growth Model. The story behind the creation of the infrastructure will need to wait until Book 3: change to LIVE better & LEAD differently, which is scheduled for release in April 2020. For now, here is a sneak peek at the finished design. See Illustration #6: The Model for Balanced Change below.

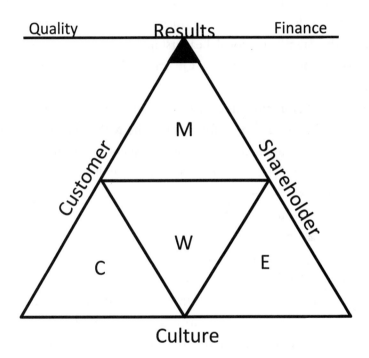

The infrastructure is made up of four, interconnected, interdependent triangles. Forming the majority of the support structure for the Culture are: "C" which stands for Communication and "E" which represents Education. At the top, spearheading the Model for Balanced Change, is "M", Motivation. And, in the center and acting as the glue holding it all together is "W", Why. No matter what the change and no matter how big or how small, successfully leading transformation is always dependent on the Core understanding "Why." Much, much more on the interworkings of these elements will be found in Book 3.

"How do cultures learn and develop?" Answer: "By improving on their ability to anticipate future results." The perceptions held by the customer base and shareholder group result in Cultural *choices* which reflect the changing *needs* of the Core. We know, from the previous section, that human *choices* and *needs*, individual and collective, have a profound influence on the progression of development within the Cycle. All three pieces, the Cycle, human *choices* and *needs,* and the Core, work together to form the Transformational Leadership Model. We will explore this final model when we answer Life Question #5: "How do you transform a culture?"

Usually, at about this time in the teaching process, I get questions from the audience stemming from either the MB story or the RB-KY story, depending on which illustration I have chosen to share. The audience's questions will take many forms, but they will all fall into two basic categories: "How did you know you were right?" and "Did you ever consider what would have happened if you were wrong?" These two questions, when boiled down to their essence, are really asking: "How do you determine what is true?" After all, if someone can consistently deliver to a leader the actual facts (what is really true), it is easy to make great decisions all day, every day with minimal risk of failure. This simple question brings us to the very heart of the leadership puzzle. Actually, it brings us to one of the central questions in life itself: "What is truth?"

Life Question #3
WHAT IS TRUTH?

If you are expecting a lengthy, deeply philosophical answer to this question, you will be disappointed. Much of my life has been spent helping others to perceive intangibles, like truth, as something they can grasp and grow to understand. I have made a career out of simplifying the complex, causing the intangible to appear tangible, and turning the theoretical into the practical. My basic approach has always been to help teach others by peeling back the shroud of mystery surrounding leadership through the use of transparency. Why do I approach teaching leadership in this way, helping others to live better and lead differently? Respect. Leadership Rule #1: "Always be professional, which begins with respect for yourself and everyone around you."

The go-to saying that I use when illustrating transparency to an audience is: "Pull back the flap on the tent, and let them look inside." That means I am about to take the mystery out of the process. Squash the rumors. Replace assumptions with facts and reduce the fear of the unknown by providing access to an increased Universe of Present Facts. But, and there

Pull back the flap on the tent, and let them look inside.

is a but, don't be stupid about it. That is one of the reasons why there is Leadership Rule #2: "Always strive to work smarter, not harder." Like all three Leadership Rules, there are multiple layers of meaning for these words. In this instance, working smarter means to know your audience. Do everything you can, before you step up front and lead, to understand their level of development along the Cycle, their *choices* and *needs,* and their Core responsibilities before you "pull the flap back." Respectfully, working smarter helps others to learn the truth.

Let's go back to the Transformational Conversation and my description of the initial meeting with the MB employees. When I was relaying the circumstances surrounding that evening, I shared with you the actual results but not all the facts. Now is a good time to fill in some of the missing pieces.

Remember when I sat off to the side of the room and observed the MB employees as they arrived for the meeting: "so I could watch the body language as they entered the room...facial expressions... I was looking for any clue regarding their current mindset... the group was clearly tense and apprehensive."

Now recall, from our discussion of the Cycle, my illustration framed by the scene from the movie *The Secret of My Succe$s.* I had spent hours upon hours preparing for this deal with MB in general, and for this meeting in particular. I understood as much about existing conditions and expectations within the MB culture as I could know right up to the start of the meeting. However, in that moment sitting off to the side observing, I was still learning. I was adding more facts to my Universe of Present Facts in an attempt to add to my knowledge base to be better prepared to deliver substantive communication to the people in front of me.

The nugget of critical information I was seeking came not in the form of what I was able to observe, but rather by what I did not witness through my pre-meeting observation of the MB employees. Based on my knowledge and experience, I expected to observe some level of anger and maybe some outward signs of aggression, bordering on contempt toward any RB representative. Why would I expect to see these types of behavior? If I were one of the MB proof department employees and I had just learned that I was going to lose my job, my reaction would be one of anger. Think of it this way, their foundational human *need* for security had just been placed into question. Of course, they were going to have a strong, negative reaction to the change.

The anticipated emotions were not on display. Why was that? The answer is unknown. But, in that moment, while sitting off to the side watching folks file in, my assumption was that the MB employees had not yet been told of the anticipated reduction in force resulting from this transaction. What was I going to do? Answer: be myself. Step in front of the group, raise my hand, own the results (current and future), and offer them the respect they deserved. If I were able to connect with the group in those opening moments, I had a good chance of discovering what was really going on within the MB culture during the Q&A session. And discover I did.

The first question was the key: *"Am I going to lose my job?"* The sincere nature of that question told me that we had been successful in establishing the beginnings of a productive relationship. I answered the question directly but with empathy. Then I stopped talking, allowing a respectful amount of time for my answer to be processed by the group. The strategic pause was my way of trolling for the next level of discovery. If, for example, I had chosen to immediately launch into the standard corporate gibberish, explaining the concepts behind the economies of scale to the group, the future success of the transaction would have been put at risk. Their trust in me and my integrity, two of the three elements necessary to form a productive relationship, would have been immediately called into question.

No, the group needed a moment to process what they had just heard, summon the courage, and formulate the next question. Thankfully, when the next question came, it contained the critical piece of information I was missing. I learned that the group had been told by their regional manager that no MB employee was going to lose their job as a result of the pending transaction, which was not true. Now was the right time to "pull back the flap on the tent" and let them see inside. After discovering this last nugget, I had enough information to be effectively transparent.

Within a massive organization the size of MB, miscommunication was a familiar experience. I attributed the incorrect information to a misunderstanding by telling the group:*"…I imagine it is more likely a miscommunication that occurred somewhere between the MB executives that negotiated this deal and the MB manager that delivered the message. This type of thing happens all the time."*

Just prior to offering the group this explanation for the sudden change in their perception of security, I laid out the details of my involvement in all aspects of the transaction. This level of transparency was necessary in order for me to re-affirm trust and demonstrate purpose and integrity. How did I know that our first meeting with MB employees was successful? The nature of the postmeeting questions confirmed it.

Recall when I mentioned that I knew the meeting went well because almost all of the questions after the meeting were for Anna and Jill? I could make that observation not due to the specific subjects of their questions, but rather due to the scope of their questions. Basically, all of the questions for Anna and Jill focused on the operational details related to the future. A culture in transformation is focused on the future and not on the past. If the post-meeting group had surrounded me and continued to pepper me with questions about "Why?" and "Who?" I would have known that their focus was still on the past, not on the future, signaling that the process of cultural transformation had not yet begun.

Now, I want to pause for a moment and ask you to consider what you have learned from these last few pages. You have been given a peek inside the tent. Has my going back and connecting these seemingly unrelated events, by weaving in an increased level of transparency, given you a new perspective of this meeting? What were, hopefully, interesting and stand-alone sections of this book have now been re-assembled in a new way. This new way of viewing these events has brought into focus new facts, new tools,

Always be curious and never stop learning!

new information, more knowledge, and a deeper level of understanding regarding this brief moment in time. My goodness, can you imagine the opportunities for learning we are presented with each and every day? If we only knew how to see (perceive) the opportunities around us. You can grow to better see these opportunities for learning by working smarter. Learn how to discover, daily, as many new facts as you can. Always be curious and never stop learning!

What is truth?—<u>Facts</u>

You will discover that some facts are true and some facts are false. Some facts start out as true, only to be proven false. The stove is always hot, unless it has been turned off for a while. Considering the MB story from above, do you now know <u>the truth</u> regarding this event? Answer: you now know more of what <u>is true</u> regarding the MB meeting. We are going to discover that assumed absolutes like what is true are actually variable, and the product of acceptance and perception. The Life Question: "What <u>is truth</u>?" is a completely different question than: "What is <u>the truth</u>?" To successfully lead cultural transformation, you need to develop a firm understanding of how these two questions fit into the leadership process.

Remember my story about the RB-KY negotiations? When the lead attorney turned around, walked back to where I was standing, and asked: "Rob,

> *"What <u>is truth</u>?" is a completely different question than: "What is <u>the truth</u>?"*

what do you need?" he had chosen his words carefully. A skilled attorney, he understood and respected the meaning of words, be they written or spoken. His question "What do you need?" carried a drastically different meaning than the more carelessly constructed question of: "What do you want?" Knowing the definition of the words being used is only one aspect of the fact-gathering process. One must learn the intended meaning, or the substance of the word, when in pursuit of truth.

When the toddler first hears the word "hot," it carries no particular meaning. The child has no context for the word. If the child touches the stove, he recoils from the pain and hears a parent say: "Hot! Don't touch!" The result of this sequence of events is an immediate association of the intangible (the word "hot") with the tangible (the sensation of pain). Once that association is made and the experience has effectively transferred the knowledge, the word "hot" has been granted meaning. Hot has gained the status of a fact and has earned inclusion into the toddler's Universe of Present Facts. We know from our study of the Cycle that the toddler will now progress through multiple learning loops discovering the variables associated with hot and the causes behind those variables.

The lead attorney's deliberate choice of the word "need"; my knowing how to modify the presentation to the MB employees in the last minute, based solely on observing their nonverbals; and, the toddler's ability to grasp the concept of hot are all examples of truth. More specifically, they are examples of what <u>truth is</u>. There is a huge difference between the process of discovering <u>the truth</u> and seeking to learn what <u>truth is</u>. Let's start by constructing an understanding of what truth is. **Truth is created when facts are perceived as acceptable by the individual or the culture.** Pretty straightforward. We can simplify what truth is even further by expressing it in the form of a "teaching equation": **Truth = acceptable perceived facts**. FYI: Used in tandem with illustrations, I have found that expressing complex leadership concepts in the form of

> *<u>Truth is</u> created when facts are perceived as acceptable by the individual or the culture. Truth = acceptable perceived facts.*

teaching equations is an excellent method to improve association and enhance transferability. Would you like to see the teaching equation for <u>the truth</u>? Okay, here you go: **The Truth = the sum of ({Experienced Facts} + {Proven Facts} + {Believed Facts}).**

The teaching equation for the truth is a little bit of an oversimplification, but it serves as a beginning point for understanding the differences between the two concepts. Teaching equations are used as vehicles to help frame a leadership discussion around an ever-changing intangible like what is truth versus what is the truth. In this case, the purpose of the two equations is to help leaders better understand the processes involved in discovering the truth. Much like our earlier comparison of weather forecasting as an aid to help better understand the influences on culture, the use of teaching equations is a way for us to illustrate complex concepts like truth.

$$The\ Truth = the\ sum\ of\ (\{Experienced\ Facts\} + \{Proven\ Facts\} + \{Believed\ Facts\})$$

Now, "What is truth?" We have boiled the teaching equation down to three words. Each word needs our attention so we can better understand the importance of their selection. The first two words, acceptable and perceived, serve as qualifiers for the subject facts. Let's begin with the subject word and then work our way back through the qualifiers. As we explore the underlying meaning of what truth is, we will be contrasting it to the truth.

Point number one, facts do not always equal truth. It is time for another illustrative story.

I grew up on a farm in central West Virginia. My last four years at home were challenging, but prior to that period of time, life was pretty predicable. During late spring, all summer, and through early fall, the days for my elder brother and me consisted of two things, work and school. Our sister was off attending college during these years. Our usual routine from late fall through early spring consisted of work, school, and hunting. This was normal hunting on the farm, not the travel to Montana or Africa type of hunting.

In West Virginia, the Monday before Thanksgiving signaled the start of deer season. For my brother, my dad, and most of WV, the first day of deer season was practically a national holiday on a par with Thanksgiving. Prior to the big day, my brother would spend every spare minute in the woods, hunting squirrel and looking for fresh deer signs. He and Dad would spend hours speculating on the current paths taken by the biggest bucks and planning where they would stand, waiting for the perfect buck to appear on that first morning. I listened. I went in the woods to hunt because that is what I was expected to do. There was never any discussion about it. I was a male child and as such, I worked outside in the summer and then hunted in the fall. End of discussion.

Don't get me wrong, I enjoyed hunting, especially hunting game birds. I had developed the skills needed to hunt successfully; I just didn't share my brother's and my dad's burning sense of purpose for deer hunting. When I went in the woods hunting deer, my results were never as good as my brother's. He would always come home with more food for the table than I. At the time, I was in my early teens and had not shot my first buck. Within our family culture, my failure at deer hunting was perceived as some type of significant character flaw. Season after season, my brother and Dad would get their deer early on the opening day and spend the rest of the first day putting me in the perfect spot. Time after time, year after year, at the end of the day, I would come into the house without a deer. After the fever of the first day subsided, I would be free to grab a rifle and a game bag and head into the woods on my own. I had my favorite spots, and depending on the time of day, I would head to one of those places, sit down, and wait.

While seated, I would dutifully watch and listen for the elusive buck deer to pass my way. In a few minutes, my mind would begin to wander, and I would become caught up in my thoughts or just sit and enjoy the nature around me. Shoot, I can't tell you how many times I just sat there and watched the deer walk by. It became a type of game for me. How still could I sit, and how close would the deer get to where I was sitting before they discovered my presence and trotted off?

Sometimes, during these solo excursions into the woods, I would sneak a pencil and some paper into my game bag and sketch or, on rare occasions, do some homework from school. This was one of those rare occasions when a homework assignment was the task at hand. I was in the seventh grade, and it was the weekend after Thanksgiving. One of my teachers had given us a writing assignment. When we came back from the holiday break, we were to turn in a poem written about Christmas. There were no restrictions on the Christmas-related topic, just write a poem about Christmas.

I found my spot. I unloaded my rifle, leaned it up against the tree, pulled my paper and pencil out of my game bag, and began to write. I had never written a poem before and found the creative process to be less painful than I had expected. I wrote something about how: "Santa Claus could be found in every store on the first, second, and third floors." That's all I remember about the poem itself. Hey, it wasn't much, but I was happy with my work and enjoyed the creative process. That evening, I finished the poem and proceeded to enjoy another unsuccessful deer season.

When we returned to school the following Monday, the class turned in the assignment and fell back into the routine that is seventh grade. Later that week, the teacher, a seasoned teacher with many years of classroom experience and a real no-nonsense disciplinarian, began class by calling up each student to receive their graded poems. She asked a couple of the kids to read their poems in front of the room so we could all hear a "good" poem. I waited anxiously for my name to be called. I enjoyed this assignment more than I had expected. But, did the teacher think my paper was any good? The facts surrounding her thoughts were just about to be revealed to me and to everybody in the class.

The teacher called my name, and I made my way to the front of the class. She handed me my paper, and my heart sank. There, on the top of my paper and written in red ink with a big circle around it was an "F." As if that wasn't enough, she then proceeded to tell the class that I had been given an "F" because I clearly had copied my poem out of a book and cheaters don't deserve a passing grade.

I was both embarrassed and devastated. While standing in front of her desk, I attempted to explain that I had written the poem on my own, but she cut me off and told me to go back to my desk and think about what I had done. Class went on. The school week ended. On the following Monday, she announced to the class that our grades from last week's poem assignment would be used for extra credit, whatever that meant. The bottom line was my failing grade would not hurt my overall score in the class, but it wasn't going to help me either. Experience noted. Lessons learned. Life goes on.

Needless to say, that was my last attempt at writing poetry. When forced, I would write the occasional essay, but I never really enjoyed it. Each time I did write, which was quite frequent as my leadership responsibilities grew, I would anxiously await my grade from the board of directors, the auditors, the regulators, and especially the audiences. Up until a couple years ago, when I sat down to begin the process of creating these books, I had only written for business and teaching purposes. My wife was the one who told me to "go write your book." It was her confidence that enabled me to sit down and finally put my doubts aside.

My goodness, that was a long way around the barn in order to make a few points. But, what a golden opportunity to learn and, ultimately, to teach. I have so many reasons to be grateful to that teacher for the life lessons she provided. And, before you start thinking the obvious regarding her treatment of a junior high school student, remember that these events all took place in the early 1970s. It was a different time. The culture was certainly different than our culture today. Granted, there was no excuse for the way she handled the situation, but there was a motivating purpose behind what she did. We'll touch on her motivation in a minute. This is another one of those times, just like with the MB meeting, that there was more going on here than first meets the eye.

I am grateful to her for providing such a great illustration of the difference between <u>the truth</u> and what <u>truth is</u>. <u>The truth</u> was that I created the poem on my own. Fact: I had not cheated. Fact: I did not copy someone else's work. Fact: I received a failing grade and a stern rebuke from the teacher. The <u>truth is</u> she perceived my poem as being copied, and she accepted her conclusion as fact. After all, she had my paper in hand. Fact: No seventh grader, at least none that she had taught, would write a poem like that without copying it. The <u>truth is</u> the conclusion that I copied the poem was an acceptable perception for the teacher. Do you see the difference? Truth = acceptable perceived facts where The Truth = the sum of ({Experienced Facts} + {Proven Facts} + {Believed Facts}). All I had on my side of the truth equation were Experienced Facts. I was there. I knew what happened. But, I could offer no Proven Facts to bolster my argument and she was certainly not going to believe my offering of facts.

The truth is the teacher was willing to accept the facts as she perceived them and act on those acceptable perceived facts. The actual result, the truth, was I got an "F." If you haven't learned this already, you will eventually. The notion is wrong that <u>the truth</u> will always prevail because it is "right." The acceptable perception of what <u>truth is</u> will be acted upon in the moment, even though it may be proven to be wrong in the future. As a leader tasked with transforming a culture, your mission is to match up, as closely as possible, what <u>truth is</u> (acceptable perceived facts) with <u>the truth</u> (provable facts generated from actual results influenced by firmly held belief).

> *The acceptable perception of what <u>truth is</u> will be acted upon in the moment, even though it may be proven to be wrong in the future.*

Before we leave this Life Lesson and expand our understanding of facts, perception, and acceptability , allow me to pull back the flap on the tent and share some additional information. When I came home with my grade for the class just before Christmas break, I knew there would be a price to pay. During that grading period, I had received a B- (B minus) for the class, which my dad perceived as a failing grade. His reaction was swift and the conclusion was obvious; I was just being lazy. Both he and Mom were sitting in the room with me during this review of my grades. I was usually not permitted to speak during this type of session, but this time I just had to plead my case. After I had told my story, Mom asked Dad: "Is she the one?" to which Dad replied: "Yes." That was all that was said on the subject. (FYI: This is adult code for "we'll talk about it later.") The pronouncement was (truth is) I was just being lazy and I had better get an "A" in that class for the next grading period.

At the time, Dad was the superintendent of schools for the WV county in which we lived. Believe me when I say that he was the person in charge. A nationally recognized leader in secondary school administration, Dad was a fierce advocate for the children in his system. He was a skilled practitioner of Maximum Command and Control and possessed a finely honed ability to get his point across. Several years later, long after Dad had retired, I was having an unrelated conversation with my mother when I learned that about a week before I turned in my poem, my teacher, along with the principal, had been summoned to my dad's office. I have no idea about the reason for the meeting with Dad, but based on personal experience, I assume the conversation was not a pleasant one for my teacher. The seventh grade me, along with my first attempt at creative writing, just happened to get caught up in a grown-up issue. My poem and I were collateral damage. Oh well, that's life. Learn from the experience and move on.

How can I dismiss this event so easily? Perception. I choose to see this experience and so many more as opportunities to learn.

> *The truth was my future had not been written, and I was in control of my own perception of the facts.*

Actually, I am very grateful to the teacher, not only for providing me with an excellent example for this book, but for the learning opportunity, another Life Lesson. About four years after seventh grade, my life circumstances at home on the farm would become challenging. I would be faced with the choice of accepting Dad's frequent and forceful opinions of me as being lazy, worthless, and having no future or choosing to perceive his relentless reminders differently. I chose to perceive his opinions of me in a manner similar to those opinions I held regarding my seventh grade teacher. Just like she was wrong about me, Dad was also wrong about me. I credit those seventh grade lessons with providing the understanding that people, even adults, can be flat wrong. Through her actions, the teacher had taught me that the exact same set of facts can be perceived differently by different people. What she accepted to be true regarding my poem wasn't the truth at all. Was it possible that my dad was mistaken about my work ethic, my self-worth, and my future? Of course, it was. Truth is, Dad perceived my character as flawed and my future as bleak. The truth was my future had not been written, and I was in control of my own perception of the facts. Interesting, isn't it? There is much to be considered regarding the impact on an individual or on a culture which is driven by how those in positions of influence choose to perceive and accept a set of facts.

What is truth?—<u>Perceived</u> Facts

Truth = acceptable *perceived* facts. Working our way backward from the subject (facts) to the first qualifier (perceived), let's briefly explore the concept of perception. Two different people or two differing cultures in possession of the exact same facts may reach polar opposite conclusions. Fact: My poem was written on the same piece of paper that the teacher possessed. Fact: I wrote and she read the exact same words. How is it possible for the teacher to conclude that the words I had submitted were copied, while at the same time I knew that the words were my own? Is this a rare anomaly, experienced only once or twice in a lifetime? Heavens no. The same facts produce polar opposite truths all the time, millions of times a day.

> *The same facts produce polar opposite truths all the time, millions of times a day.*

Want proof? Every time someone buys a share of stock in a company, it is because someone else was willing to sell that same share. Two parties, the buyer and the seller, with access to the same facts regarding the same company have independently reached the exact opposite conclusions. How? Each party holds a different perception of the future value of the share. The seller perceives the greatest, future value of the share will be realized by turning it into cash and then applying that cash elsewhere. The buyer perceives the greatest, future value of their available cash will be realized by purchasing a share of the company's stock. The vast majority of these factual conflicts will take place with no one outside of the buyer and the seller being impacted. A piece of accounting software records both sides of the transaction, adjusting the appropriate asset line items on the respective balance sheets, and life goes on.

The risk to the buyer and seller from being ultimately proven right or wrong regarding the actions taken, based on their acceptable perception of the facts, is so narrow in scope that no one gives the downstream consequences a second thought. But what if you knew that your perception of the facts could ultimately cost someone or a group of people their jobs? What if you knew that the conclusions you reached on your way to determining what truth is would disrupt the lives of dozens of families, an entire community, or a nation, or shape the life of one seventh grade student? Now we are talking about real risk and significant downstream consequences. We are talking about the very real responsibility of leadership, the ability to influence a person, a family, a company, or an entire culture.

In leadership, we strive to gather as many facts as we can and perceive the facts from as many different perspectives as possible (upstream processes within the Cycle), while choosing the path most likely to reflect favorably on the *choices* and benefit the *needs* of our Core. Then, once the decision regarding truth is made, we test our information, gain knowledge from the results, and improve our level of understanding (downstream processes within the Cycle). When the path of leadership is chosen, begin each journey with your feet firmly planted on the rock of respect (Leadership Rule #1), and proceed down the path while striving to work smarter, not harder (Leadership Rule #2).

Take the information in the paragraph above and apply it to the RB/ MB example from the beginning of this book, <u>A Transformational Conversation</u>. Combine your new perception of the MB conversation with the earlier section where I pulled back the flap on the tent and provided you with additional transparency regarding that first meeting with the MB employees. Do you now perceive the exact same facts differently? How is this possible? The words (the facts) are unchanged. The change is possible because your <u>perception</u> of the words has been altered. Your <u>perspective</u> has been changed. You now have acquired the ability to "hold the prism of truth up to the light and see the different colors." (Yes, I actually use that saying as an illustration. It works. In daily practice, the wording is shortened to: "hold it up to the light.") It means take the time to consider as many differing perspectives as available, then choose the resulting perception of what truth is that best matches the purpose of your Core.

During our earlier discussion of the Cycle, there are a couple of non-descript sentences where I was talking about the ability to anticipate future events, or a leader's ability to see around the corner. These sentences read: *"Weeks and weeks of transaction-specific work, combined with years of leadership experience, developed my understanding of the transaction from both RB's perspective and MB's perspective. This is how I was able to anticipate the circumstances related to this transaction from RB's and MB's points of view. I understood the financial choices and needs of both sides, and I was able to anticipate the resulting influences on the two cultures."* These words now take on a broader and deeper meaning. You now have a better understanding of my purpose and all the work surrounding my preparation for the MB transaction. Perceptions are subject to change by evolving perspectives, which is how the same facts can equate to two different perspectives of the truth at

> *Perceptions are subject to change by evolving perspectives, which is how the same facts can equate to two different perspectives of the truth at the same time.*

the same time. The stock transaction is an example and so is watching a duck on a pond.

Picture a single duck on a pond. If you are on the shore watching the duck swim, the appearance for all the world to see is the duck gracefully, effortlessly moving forward while perched calmly on the surface of the water. Standing on the shore, the <u>perception</u> of the duck is one of calm. However, if we would change our <u>perspective</u>, not viewing the duck from the shore but rather from below the surface of the water, our perception would change from one of calm to one of frantic activity. From below the surface of the water, one would witness the duck's feet working feverishly just to keep progressing forward. The greater the headwinds, the invisible forces of resistance, blowing against the duck, the harder it works in order to make progress toward its destination.

There are many critical leadership lessons to be gleaned from this simple example. Let's begin by defining the two words: perception and perspective. "Perception" is defined as: an act of perceiving—consciousness; a result of perceiving—observation; a mental image; awareness of the elements of the environment through physical sensation; physical sensation interpreted in the light of experience; and a capacity for comprehension. In short, perception is your ability to view the duck (the facts) from where you are standing.

"Perspective" is defined as: the interrelation in which a subject or its parts are mentally viewed and the capacity to view things in their true relations or relative importance. Perspective is the place you choose to be when viewing the duck.

These two words share one common synonym, the world view. Truly understanding yourself or the culture around you begins when you learn to view the world from multiple perspectives in an effort to perceive the world as it truly exists. This is "holding it up to the light."

Please notice that I used the words "view the world," not "see the world." This subtle choice in the words opens the door of opportunity for us to experience life-altering change. First, you are only able to view the opportunity after learning to see the duck from <u>both</u> the shore and from under the water, simultaneously. Example, view the opportunities presented by the transaction from both the buyer's side and the seller's side. Only then will you have learned to respect the duck for its ability to project a calm, purposeful demeanor, while appreciating the unrelenting effort needed for it to keep moving forward at the same time. This equates to the leader's ability to simultaneously view a culture's conditions (environmental and economic), while understanding the perspective they hold (expectations) regarding their accepted facts.

My seventh grade teacher's view led her to conclude that I had plagiarized my poem, when I knew I had not. MB's executive group knew that it was the right time to sell their branches while, in that same moment, RB's executive team decided it was a good time to buy those same locations. These are two examples of a set of facts perceived differently from varying perspectives and resulting in polar opposite truths. We now know "how" this is possible but "why" does this happen? The why is because truth = *acceptable* perceived facts.

What is truth?—<u>Acceptable</u> Perceived Facts

We understand "how" an identical set of facts can be perceived differently, resulting in two parties simultaneously reaching polar opposite conclusions. For us to understand "why" this happens, we need to return to the beginning of the Cycle of Human Development (Cycle). We need to focus our attention on the Universe of Present Facts (Present Facts). Present Facts are those facts which are both current and existing. The word "present" has two very different meanings. One meaning for present is "current." Within the context of the Cycle, current simply means readily available to you through some type of automated or manual discovery process. A second meaning for present is "existing." Facts change as knowledge changes. The facts which are acceptable today exist and can be disproven and removed tomorrow. Present Facts, current and existing, constantly evolve as do the methods available for us to access, sort, and extract them.

Just because a fact is present and discoverable does not make it correct. Illustration #7 shows the top section of the Cycle only, depicting the body of Present Facts and the search engines used to deliver user-defined data.

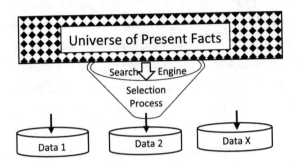

To better understand the process of acceptability, we need to enhance our model of the Cycle to include the critically important Universe of Absent Facts (Absent Facts) in Illustration #8 below.

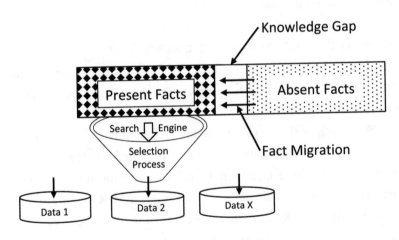

The use of the word "absent" also carries a dual meaning. First, an Absent Fact can be a fact that is known (discoverable) but lies beyond your current scope of knowledge. For example, a fact regarding the function of the human body which is known to the trained physician but unknown to me, is absent but discoverable, remaining unknown until I become curious. Only when I choose to seek the unknown fact will it migrate through the knowledge gap. Once the migration is complete, I can choose to select the new fact, causing it to become part of my learning and development process.

When we are very young, we learn at an incredible rate. The pace at which individual facts migrate from Absent Facts to Present Facts is staggering. The first time a toddler touches a hot stove, bang, the concept of stove = hot = pain is immediately transferred from the Absent into the Present. As we age, approaching our mid-teens, the chemical processes related to puberty begin to take hold, and the pace of transfer between the two universes slows. During this period, what we have learned is locked, encoded into our brains serving as our universe of the known, Present Facts. To borrow a phrase from one of my favorite *Star Wars* characters, Yoda: "Already know you that which you need."

Deal with any young adult and the phrase, "I know that" is a common response to any comment made by a parent. In their minds, they do "know." The good news is that for these young adults, the human *choice* of curiosity, combined with the passage of time, will open new avenues for the migration of discoverable facts from the Absent to the Present. Those of us who are chronologically older place a label on this migration process and call it: maturity.

The second meaning for absent relates to those facts which are, at that moment in time, both unknown and/or undiscoverable. Unknown and/or undiscoverable facts can reference information that may exist but remains out of reach to an individual or culture due to their unique environmental and economic conditions. The Knowledge Gap is what separated the culture of the Haves from the culture of the Have-nots. Then there is a set of undiscoverable facts which reside beyond the grasp of all humanity. Examples of these types of facts are: a cure for all cancers, discovering the origins of the universe, or the existence of God?

Here is where the concepts behind Present and Absent Facts get really interesting. How do Present and Absent Facts relate to our growing understanding of: "What is truth?" and "What is the truth?" Recall our equations: Truth = acceptable perceived facts and, The Truth = the sum of ({Experienced Facts} + {Proven Facts} + {Believed Facts}). Truth is created at a point in time when the accumulation of acceptable perceived facts meets the threshold of being actionable: "That is good enough; I know what I need to know in order to move forward and take action."

The stove is hot; don't touch it. The poem was clearly copied, so give the student a failing grade. Now is the time for RB to purchase the branches from MB and they are worth X amount of money. These three are all examples of actions which occurred after the accumulation of acceptable perceived facts reached the point of making a choice. Truth is actionable and is based on Present Facts. Actions based on what is true will be proven to be either right or wrong over a period of time. When we touch the hot stove or assess the meaning of nonverbals displayed by others in a meeting, we will immediately receive feedback to determine if our actions were right or wrong. If truth is what leads one company to purchase another, it may be months or even years before it is finally known if the right choice of action was taken or not. Acceptable perceptions form the basis for an individual's or culture's call to action.

The truth is a result. Regardless of the result being perceived as acceptable or as unacceptable, the result is the result. The truth is the truth. Examples: Pain results from touching a stove when it is hot; the actual facts had no bearing on my being given a failing grade for the poem; and RB's purchase of MB's branches made money in the first year of operation. These three events are all examples of Experienced Facts, the first factor in The Truth equation.

> *Truth is actionable and is based on Present Facts.*
> *The truth is a result.*

The truth is also made up of Proven Fact. If I have two apples on the table and I put two more apples on the table with them, I now have a total of four apples. Proven Facts, not facts which are acceptable and present, equate to <u>the truth</u>. Facts that can be tested over and over again and always return the same results are Proven Facts. That is why pain resulting from touching a hot stove is an Experienced Fact and not a Proven Fact. One may touch the stove several times when it is not hot and experience no pain. Proven Facts are typically rooted in mathematics and the sciences.

Then, there is the third factor in The Truth equation: Believed Facts. This is where the truth equation gets very interesting. Experienced Facts and Proven Facts reside almost exclusively in the Universe of Present Facts. Believed Facts are Absent Facts. Most Believed, Absent Facts are discoverable over the course of a lifetime. A toddler who has never touched a hot surface believes his parent's warnings, but when he actually comes into contact with hot, the truth switches from Believed status to Experienced status. <u>The truth</u> is still the truth; it has just migrated from the Absent to the Present.

But what about that second group of undiscovered facts which currently reside beyond the grasp of all humanity? Is it human nature to simply accept the currently unknown as undiscoverable? Of course not. The *choices* of curiosity and courage, combined with the ever-changing *need* for purpose, will constantly drive human exploration of the unknown, migrating Absent Facts into the Present. Allow me to ask you this: Do you believe that the human *choice* of curiosity is the sole motivation for the scientist that spends their entire life's work in an effort to discover the undiscoverable? Was it curiosity alone that caused the discovery of a cure for polio or expands our understanding of the universe? Most people would answer these questions with a resounding: "no" followed by a valid explanation pointing out that these discoveries and countless others are examples of the indomitable human spirit. Over the course of human history, intelligence guided by experience, coupled with new technologies, a dedication to a cause (a purpose), and faith have combined with curiosity and courage to produce life-altering results (truths).

Now, revisit the previous sentence and find the word that is uniquely human. The single word that separates mankind from all other known species of life is "faith." Faith is the uniquely human ability to choose to perceive that undiscoverable facts, the most elusive members of the set labeled as Absent Facts, are somehow discoverable and, as such, are to be viewed as the truth. I think we can all agree that faith has been and will always be a huge influence on all aspects of the Cycle of Human Development. But, can we all agree that the faith driving the research scientist to discover the cure for cancer is the same faith which enables a Christian to believe in a life after death?

Pick any scientific discipline or religious teaching. I chose to reference the Christian teaching in my question to you because it is the most familiar to me. The examples I used to establish the contrast are irrelevant; however, the point is undeniable. The research scientist, the priest, the farmer, or the CEO are all drawing on the same faith in the pursuit of Absent Facts.

> *The research scientist, the priest, the farmer, or the CEO are all drawing on the same faith in the pursuit of Absent Facts.*

The word "faith" is defined as: firm belief in something for which there is no proof. Unfortunately, we have allowed faith to be redefined as a human failing afflicting only a small group of people, causing them to mistakenly perceive certain facts as the truth. Continuing with this ridiculous scenario, the obvious conclusion is that faith should not be allowed to spread to the rest of the population.

Once faith is permitted to be defined through the use of this narrow application, it can be easily isolated and systematically removed for the good of the broader culture. Sound familiar? I told you our exploration of truth was going to get interesting. I submit to you that The Truth equation must remain unchanged. The truth is derived from both Present and Absent Facts. The uniquely human ability to have faith in the undiscoverable is a benefit we ALL share, including the research scientist and the priest. To allow the removal of faith from the human experience is to allow the restriction of truth, changing The Truth equation to read: The Truth = ({Experienced Facts} + {Proven Facts} + {Acceptable Facts}). Changing the factor of Believed Facts to Acceptable Facts removes individuality from The Truth equation. Removing faith removes innovation and individual freedom from the culture. The individuality of belief is replaced with the cultural determination of what Acceptable Facts are and are not. This creates the environment for two differing cultures, the Haves and the Have-nots. The results are an ever-widening communication gap, increasing restrictions on the migration of Absent Facts into the Present, which slows or completely stops cultural development.

How does this happen? How can the natural Cycle of Human Development and the resulting cultural advancements be restricted to the point of actually being controlled? Answer: Through the use of ideology. Our discussion of ideology, its impact on cultural development, and the use of results to counter its effect take off in the next section: Life Question #4 – What is ideology and how does it impact culture?

How does this discussion of what truth is (actions taken based on acceptable perceived facts) versus the truth (experienced, proven, and believed results) impact cultural transformation? Remember on the ride back home from the MB meeting when Anna explained to Jill that the accepted practice in a pre-acquisition presentation of this type was to always avoid direct answers to direct questions. She went on to say that she had never seen anyone commit to taking responsibility for future results, much less taking responsibility in advance for all those things that will almost certainly go wrong during the course of something as complicated as an acquisition. Anna's response to Jill summarizes two cultural applications of truth.

If I had stepped up in front of the group and delivered the typical list of acceptable perceived facts, I would have been positioning myself to <u>transition</u> the culture, not transform it. Examples of acceptable facts in this type of meeting are: the closing date of the merger is expected to be X date; the shareholder vote approving the merger is expected to take place on X date; the addition of the new locations will grow RB's asset base to Y dollars; RB has been a locally owned bank in the region for Z number of years; etc. You get the idea. This is the same type of information Mr. E, RB's CEO, provided to RB-KY's attorneys at the end of the failed negotiation session. These facts were, most likely, not known by the audience, which would make them of some value to the listeners. These were statements of fact, which are true at that moment in time and served to facilitate the transition of Absent Facts into Present Facts within the cultures being addressed. They were safe comments, well within acceptable corporate practice, and factually accurate. This standard approach is a call for action, transitioning the culture from one which executes the policies and procedures of MB to one that executes RB's policies and procedures. Following these acceptable practices certainly generates less risk to the leader, but it is very restrictive on the potential growth of the culture, and curtails future development.

I, on the other hand, had chosen to address the MB group with <u>the truth</u>. My words specifically conveyed commitments to future results. I was calling for the group to believe in future events while, at the same time, establishing a new set of future cultural expectations. I assumed all risk of any failure resulting from their willingness to believe by personally taking the responsibility (accepting the consequences) for any future negative results. At the same time, I committed to pass the credit for any future positive results on to them. To add credibility to my statements, I provided a level of informational transparency and personal respect that was in sharp contrast to their current cultural norms. This was a risky, nonstandard approach for delivering the truth. This method was focused on a call for achieving future results, <u>transforming</u> the culture from one which executed the policies and procedures of MB to one that believed in RB's vision for the future. A call to understand and support RB's policies and procedures as well as share our focus on the Core. Yes, the risk was much greater but the future rewards were unrestricted. The potential growth of the culture was limited only by the skill and courage of RB's leaders and the *choices* and *needs* of the population.

Do you see the differences in the application of what is truth versus the application of the truth? Think about when the RB-KY lead attorney asked me what I needed. Given what we now know, it is clear that he was really asking me to list for him the future results that were needed by the RB Core. He and I had spent the entire day listening to others argue over "what is truth." His question was really an invitation for me to join him in a discussion of the truth. It took courage to ask the question and courage, along with a solid commitment to purpose, to answer the question.

As we wrap up this section regarding truth, allow me to take you back to the airplane and the creation of the Balanced Growth Model. Recall that I needed to create a dynamic model which was a way to illustrate the changing demands of customers and shareholders and project the impact to future results (Quality and Financial). This model enabled me to challenge the audience, asking them to design cultural changes to re-balance the Results Line after witnessing the impact of the Core's new demands. Using this model, I was able to teach within a transformational environment, focusing the audience on future results and not on historic or current actions.

Leading cultural transformation depends on the strategic application of full transparency, coupled with

> *Leading cultural transformation depends on the strategic application of full transparency, coupled with the focus on results (the truth).*

the focus on results (the truth). When used properly, these two transformational leadership cornerstones (transparency and results) will facilitate a massive and rapid migration of Absent Facts into Present Facts, accelerating cultural development. The third foundational cornerstone of cultural transformation is facilitating unrestricted access to all manner of search engines and informational tools in order to encourage progression along the Cycle. It is wise for leaders to encourage the use of leadership tools like the Natural Ratio and The Most Important Person In The Room (from Book 1). And always, always remember the most powerful tool for learning is the question, represented by the Cycle's learning loop. Successfully leading cultural transformation is not so much dependent on what is known as it is dependent on the leader's ability to recognize what is not known. Your mother was right: "All you have to do is ask." I will tell you to always be questioning what you think you know, and then, once you ask the right question, shut up long enough to learn. Then, ask the next, better question. Never stop learning!!

Life Question #4
WHY?

This is a good spot for us to take a brief pause from learning about the "How" and "Why" related to the cultural transformation process. Take a moment to ask yourself these fundamental questions: "Why are these books written using so many personal life experiences?"; "Why is this the first time I have seen information like this when no one else writes this way?"; and the biggest question of all, "Why is this information important to me?"

Up to this point in Book 2 and all through Books one and three (Book 3 has a scheduled release date of spring 2020), I have shared my personal experiences, using them as a vehicle for delivering a simple but important message. The message is: "I am not special. My life experiences are not unlike yours. I have known what it is like to succeed beyond my wildest dreams and what it means to fail miserably. We have all experienced the lessons offered by our successes and failures in life. The key to living better and leading differently is how we choose to perceive those lessons. We must understand that opportunities

> *The key to living better and leading differently is how we choose to perceive the lessons offered by our successes and failures in life.*

for learning are presented to us every day around the kitchen table, in the boardroom, and at points in-between." Does any success I may have mean I am better than you, or was I just lucky? Does failure mean I am somehow less worthy than you, or was it just bad timing? I like telling the following story to illustrate the answers to these two questions. When I tell it, this story never fails to connect with members of the audience. Here is the tale of Og and Grog.

One morning Og, the strongest and smartest caveman in the tribe, saw a round boulder roll down the hillside, and he got to thinking: "That fun. Others like." So Og went down to the bottom of the hill and rolled the rock back up the hill to his part of the cave. After securing a secluded spot, Og began working on an idea. Rolling the heavy rock up the hill took all of Og's strength. The first thing he set out to do was to make the rock lighter. By making the rock lighter, all the members of the tribe, not just the strongest, could have a chance to enjoy rolling it down the hill. Og chiseled one side of the rock, removing some of the weight. When he tested the lighter rock to see how it rolled, there was still too much weight, and it didn't roll as well as it did originally. He went back to the cave for more work.

Og pondered on his dilemma for a day or two and decided to chisel away the other side of the rock. That seemed to work. The rock had less weight, and it rolled better. Now the rock was circular with two flat sides. Again, Og took a couple of days to think about his creation. He decided to cut a hole in the center of the rock to get rid of even more weight. Once the work was done, Og stood in the shadow of the flickering fire and admired his finished work. Surely the entire tribe would appreciate his work and enjoy seeing the rock magically roll down the hill.

After a week of work, the big day came, and he was ready to unveil his new magical rock to the members of the tribe. The night before the big reveal, rain had poured outside the cave, but the morning of Og's greatest success, the sky was bright blue and crystal clear. It was the perfect day for his crowning success.

Og rolled his new invention out for all to see. He had labored to produce a new form of entertainment for the tribe, and everyone was excited to see what their leader had created. Og had no words to describe the oddly shaped rock. He did, however, possess a great sense of pride regarding his work, anticipating praise and tribute from the other members of the tribe for his accomplishment. Og proudly rolled his creation out of the cave to the wonder of all that were assembled. He positioned the carved stone so it would roll down the dirt path from the entry of the cave to the bottom of the hill. He started the rock on its journey down the hill. His creation rolled about four feet and promptly got stuck in the mudhole created by the previous night's rain.

Watching in horror, Og ran up to the carved rock, which was buried about halfway in the mud, and tried to pull it free. It wouldn't budge. Other members of the tribe began to gather around the rock to help Og pull it out of the mud, but he picked up a large limb from the ground, swung it wildly above his head, and threatened to hit anyone that would dare touch his creation. The other members of the tribe, fearing a blow from Og's tree branch, stood back and watched him struggle against the weight of the stone and pull of the mud. After an hour or so, they all left Og to his work and went on with their daily routines. Night was beginning to fall, and Og, still pulling on the stone, was worn out by his struggle. Humiliated by his failure and totally exhausted, Og walked down the path, leaving the safety of the cave and the tribe, never to be heard from again.

The next morning, the new leader of the tribe, Grog, got up early and left the cave before anyone else was awake. Grog crouched alongside the path, staring at the carved rock, which was still stuck in what was now mostly dirt because the mud had begun to dry. As he pondered the situation, other members of the tribe began to gather around Grog. Grog approached the unusually shaped creation and picked up the limb that Og had used the day before to threaten others. When Grog picked up the tree branch, the tribe stepped back, remembering the previous day's lessons. He placed the stick through the hole Og had carved in the center of the rock and motioned to other members of the tribe to join him. With two men pulling on each side of the branch, the rock came out of the hole with ease.

Grog pointed to a spot on the path just beyond the mud. Still rolling the rock by using the limb, the men followed Grog's lead and maneuvered the rock to the area on the path that was dry. Grog then held the rock in place as the others removed the large stick from the center. He then released the rock. It traveled down the path, gathering speed with each rotation. The tribe stood silent in stunned amazement as the rock reached the bottom of the hill and rolled to a stop. There was a moment of silence before the tribe erupted in cheers.

What an incredible site! The tribe begged Grog to do it again, so he and the other three men took the branch down to the bottom of the hill, put it through the center hole and rolled the rock back up to where the tribe was assembled. Once the stone was properly positioned, Grog motioned to one of the men to come over to the carved rock and hold it in place. He then motioned to the man to release the rock, causing it to roll down the hill to the delight of the tribe.

The day was spent rolling the rock down the hill. Then, using the limb through the center, the men would roll it back up the hill, starting the process all over again. Each time the rock was ready to be released, Grog made certain a different member of the tribe had the opportunity to start it on its journey. The experiences shared that day brought the tribe together. They were all learning about the joy of starting the rock on its way down the hill.

One member of the tribe, Tog, Og's eldest son, was impatiently waiting his turn. As Tog stood watching the others experience the joy of letting the rock go, he had a thought: "My turn! Stand in path. Catch rock. My turn!" Brilliant, creative, and filled with confidence, much like his father, Tog leaped into action on the very next roll. Sprinting down the hill ahead of the rock, Tog stood astride the path, ready to stop the rock from traveling all the way to the bottom. As it approached where he was standing, Tog could see the rock picking up speed, rolling faster and faster. Grog, seeing what was happening, motioned to Tog to get out of the path of the rock. Tog waived Grog's offer of help off, much like his father's refusal of help the day before when he was trying to free the rock from the mud. Closer and closer the rock sped toward Tog. He mustered all of his strength as he prepared to catch the advancing stone.

Later that evening, after the tribe had buried Tog, they sat around the fire considering the lessons learned. Let's spend a moment and do the same.

There are so many leadership takeaways from this story. There are always the lessons to be learned when a leader makes the choice of arrogance over humility. Confidence is a powerful ally for a leader, but arrogance will always lead you toward walking the path exhausted and alone. Then, there is the lesson about the power of timing. Always remember, you may have the greatest idea since the invention of the wheel, but if you roll the idea out at the wrong time, your brilliant concept may very well get stuck in an environment that is not ready to favorably receive your creation. Timing is critical. Many times, it is the single most important factor in the success or failure of an idea. It could be that the environment is just not ready for the concept (Og rolling out the rock the morning after a rainstorm). It could also be that your idea is too far ahead of the current environment, and it will be rolled over and squashed by the forces in control (Tog's unfortunate experience with the power of momentum).

> *Confidence is a powerful ally for a leader, but arrogance will always lead you toward walking the path exhausted and alone.*

My sharing of experiences, be they real-life or literary creations, is designed to provide you with the feeling of familiarity, creating the ability to relate to the circumstances being described. If I can somehow make these leadership lessons personal to you, then I have succeeded in making the opportunities real as well. This is the "Why" behind the use of stories in this series. This is also why most of the material put forward in this trilogy is original to me, from the stories being offered to most of the terminology being used and from the models shown to the concepts they represent. This is how I view the world of leadership. There are opportunities for us to learn and grow everywhere, every day. The key is understanding how to hold the prism of our daily lives up to the light so that we can see the different colors hidden within each moment.

As you read the second half of this book, we will be adding to your foundational understanding of culture and cultural leadership. You will be exposed more to application than shared experiences. These models and concepts you are about to discover will become keys for you to use when unlocking your future and the future of the cultures around you. Everything you have learned and are about to learn has been designed to help you better understand how to create momentum for personal and cultural change and to help you to understand why developing these skills is so important.

If I had submitted the poem to my seventh grade teacher the week before she had the meeting with my dad, instead of the week after, would the outcome have been the same? Most likely not. If the experience would have been different, would I have gone on to a career in writing, as opposed to a career in leadership? Who knows? More importantly, if the timing of the experiences would have been different, I would have missed the life lesson which taught me the different perceptions regarding truth. A couple of years later, that lesson of perception enabled me to survive and thrive within a challenging home environment. Those skills established the foundation of my being different, giving me the ability to perceive opportunities from multiple perspectives. Timing can be everything when it comes to success or failure. Never ignore its power and never fail to learn the lessons in life it offers. Og and Tog never understood the power of timing.

In addition to illustrating the importance of timing, this story offers us a valuable lesson regarding the power of shared experience. Og wanted to save the experience for only himself and found failure. Grog wanted to share the experience and the joy with the tribe and found success. On that day, Tog was not the only member of the tribe to discover the power of momentum. Each time a member of the culture experienced the joy of starting the rock down the hill, that member gained the understanding of what it felt like to be part of a collective relationship. Each time the experience was shared, the momentum grew, along with the capacity for change within the tribe.

As the tribe sat around the fire that evening reflecting on the experiences of the day, you can bet at least one member was wondering if there were any other possible uses for the round rock with a stick through the middle of it. With the passage of generation after generation, one small idea would lead to another, which would eventually lead to the creation of the two-wheeled cart.

When similar experiences are shared, they create a bound and a feeling of familiarity. Those who share similar reference points can anticipate the actions of another, establishing the emotion of trust. Trust helps to enable the courage necessary to be curious, reducing the fear of failure which creates the capacity within each of us to try new things. Creating the capacity for risk and attempting change clears the path for additional experience. Successful experiences build more momentum and more capacity for change where experiencing failure is simply another opportunity to learn. This is why these books have been

No matter what the result, success or failure, there will always be an opportunity to learn. You just need to know how to see it.

written using the life lesson format. I needed to find a vehicle to deliver this message: "No matter what the result, success or failure, there will always be an opportunity to learn. You just need to know how to see it."

Allow me to pose a question: "Of all the lessons from the story of Og and Grog, which one best illustrates the concept of cultural transformation? Where do we find the single, most powerful example of change?

Team versus individual? Choosing dry ground as the starting point along the path?" No, the single greatest example of transformation found within this story is the use of the limb. Og grabbed the limb and used it as a weapon to threaten those offering him help. He wanted to secure any future glory for himself. After considering his options, Grog picked up that same branch and used it as a solution to the problem. It became a focus for generating the combined strength to remove the rock from the mud. It also was used to easily roll the rock back up the hill, enabling all members of the tribe to participate in the experience. The stick became part of a team building exercise, a process improvement, and a central part of the shared experience. Odds are when someone comes up with the idea for creating the two-wheeled cart, the missing piece to this revolutionary, new concept will be the expanded use of the stick. This stick, originally used as a weapon, was transformed through the use of original thought into a positive solution to a current problem. That same concept would later be transformed again through courage and curiosity into one of humanity's greatest tools, the axel. Opportunity is always available to those willing to take the time to understand, viewing it from multiple perspectives.

My goal is to provide you with new leadership tools, but more importantly, my goal is to provide you with a new perspective.

As we will learn in Book 3, nothing can stop the power of change, but there are ways to affect its progress by either slowing it to a crawl or speeding it along. Is your leadership skill set geared toward maintaining the status quo or toward facilitating growth in yourself and those around you? Your answer to this question forms the essence of your influence framing the core of your leadership. My goal is to provide you with new leadership tools, but more importantly, my goal is to provide you with a new perspective.

Every idea offered in these books is a beginning point, a solution being offered to solve a current problem and to better prepare you to overcome future challenges. The real potential benefit lies in how you choose to utilize these concepts and tools. My contribution through the writing of these books is not in providing the axel. No, I only wish to transform the "stick" (leadership) from being used as a weapon into a useful tool through the application of understanding. A lifetime of experience has taught me that understanding is best developed through: the sharing of experiences; the use of illustrations, teaching formulas, and models transforming the intangible into the tangible; the transparency of thought to foster understanding; and the courage to be different, accepting risk for the benefit of others.

Beginning with Life Question #5, the discussion around ideology, and continuing on with Life Question #6, the discussion of Our Nation's culture, you may think I am injecting my personal political views into our quest to live better and lead differently. Please allow me to establish a clear understanding for all. Our current political environment is, by far, the best example for me to use in order to draw a clear distinction between the two foundational and competing ideologies. It is the best vehicle for me to use to deliver a critical message to you and to the next generations.

Political party affiliations, conservative versus liberal, who cares? To borrow a line written by Shakespeare in his 1597 tragedy *Romeo and Juliet*: "A plague o' both your houses!" Unfortunately, in today's world, the vast majority of the people who make a living from national politics and those who make a living from following those in politics are "lost pups in the woods!" Ever seen a lost pup? They run first one way, then the other, bouncing up and down trying to see the horizon in hopes of catching a glimpse of the familiar. The pup has no plan, just perpetual, meaningless motion until the winds of fate move them in one direction or the other. Lost pups in the woods have no purpose and no sense of direction. They just react to changing emotions.

As pertaining to political affiliation, boardroom behavior, or kitchen table discussion, all of these cultures are the same. They are all composed of people and as you learned in Book 1, people are people no matter where you find them. Once you have acquired the perspective from which to view your surroundings, you will discover all cultures, regardless of size, are populated by some of the most ignorant and self-centered lost pups imaginable, as well as some of the most brilliant and caring visionaries you will ever meet. Learn from the brilliant and the caring. Help the lost pups find their way. That is why you are reading these books. You instinctively know there is more to be discovered on your leadership journey; there is understanding beyond what you have been taught up to this point. Ever seen a lost pup when they find their way home? Pure joy! That is what I am hoping for you to discover, the pure joy from understanding how to help others to lead, to learn, and to grow. This is your reward for learning—joy and a profound sense of purpose.

> *I am hoping for you to discover, the pure joy from understanding how to help others to lead, to learn, and to grow.*

To me, the contents of these next sections are about freedom, our freedom. They are about our freedom to choose, to explore, and to learn. One ideology is designed to restrict all of those inalienable human rights, and the other ideology is designed to enhance the human experience. I will reference history during our discussions because history is a great teacher. My history. Our nation's history. Ancient history. They all offer us a perspective that we would be wise to seriously consider. History provides us with the opportunity to prosper and to learn from the successes and failures of others. Shining the light of opportunity on events is not limited to just current events. Those who fail to learn from history are doomed to repeat it.

Now we turn to our discussion of ideology. Not unlike the use of the limb in the story of Og and Grog, ideology can be wielded as a weapon for restriction or used as a tool for freedom. We all need to grow in our understanding of ideology and be able to recognize it for what it is. Learn to recognize ideology when it is being used as a weapon and when it is applied as a tool. You already know that the choice of perception is ultimately yours and yours alone. Will you learn to perceive the limb's potential through Og's eyes or Grog's?

Life Question #5
WHAT IS IDEOLOGY AND HOW DOES IT IMPACT CULTURE?

Ideology is the next critical piece in our understanding of how to influence the transformation of the cultures around us. My dictionary defines ideology as: "a manner or the content of thinking characteristic of an individual, group, or culture." That's a pretty good way of defining the word ideology, but what is ideology? How can we take this critical, intangible component of culture and make it more real? Let's begin by putting ideology into leadership terms we can all relate to. Ideology is the way that leaders and cultures characteristically prioritize development, select a course of action, and establish the perception of facts.

The most direct way of expressing the teaching equation for ideology is: Ideology = Influence. I like this simple equation, but this is too concise for our purposes. Let's expand the equation a little so it reads: Ideology = Results to power of Intent. We learned during our prior discussion of truth that actual results are The Truth. The Truth = ({Experienced Facts} + {Proven Facts} + {Believed Facts}). Actual results from ideology are the accumulated impact from the leader's and culture's prioritization of development, actions taken, and perceived facts. The resulting influence from ideology can be greater than, or less than, the total impact of the actual results. This multiplying effect on results is the power of Intent.

When the actual results formed from ideology are proven to be aligned with the declared intent, then the power of intent is greater than one. In other words: "We told you up front what to expect, and now that we have completed the task, the results are what we said they would be." When aligned, declared intent and actual results serve to strengthen all elements of the Culture Model. Let's work from the inside of the Culture Model out, working from catalysts out to the external influences.

Ideology is the way that leaders and cultures characteristically prioritize development, select a course of action, and establish the perception of facts. Ideology = Results to power of Intent

We begin with the foundation of every collective relationship. The leader begins by providing substantive communication which establishes expectations. The emotion of trust is initially granted due to the influence of leadership. As progress toward the stated result is communicated, trust grows, creating more emotion and fueling expectations. With the declaration of purpose, the perception of integrity is granted, again, due to the influence of leadership. In the same way as emotion/trust, the communication of progress toward the stated intent generates growing confidence within the culture toward the integrity of purpose. Once the actual results are experienced/proven/believed by the population, then the impact on cultural conditions will be realized. At this point, every catalyst and element in the Culture Model has been positively impacted by a growth factor greater than the growth generated from just the results themselves.

Example: You woke up one morning during the middle of the winter, and your house was cold. You checked the temperature in the house, and it was fifty-two degrees, but it should have been seventy-two degrees. You called a repair person to fix your furnace and restore an acceptable temperature inside your house. You were told to expect the repair person at your house between noon and 2:00 p.m. that day. You went to work that morning and then took a half day of paid time off so you could be home to meet the repair person. When you got home at noon, the temperature in the house was down to forty-two degrees and, as you waited, the inside temperature continued to drop toward the freezing point. The 2:00 p.m. arrival time came and went with no sign of the service van and no call from the company. At 3:15 p.m., the repair person arrived. You were thrilled to show them where your furnace was located, and you left them to their work.

About ninety minutes later, they emerged and declared the furnace to be fixed. You turned the system back on and, hot dog, hot air was once again blowing out of the vents. Your household environment had been restored. The actual results were what you needed but were they what you intended?

After picking up their tools, they returned from the service van with your bill, $975! Results equaled hot air blowing again and environment was restored. But, how was your emotion of trust doing right about then? Were you feeling the integrity? I will bet your answers to both questions were decidedly negative. Why? There was no substantive communication during the entire process. There were no expectations established up front nor during the actual repair process. All you had was the required change to your environment, but because there was no declared intent, the impact on the results was a multiplying effect of less than one.

So, let's say that getting the hot air blowing again (the result) was, on a scale of priority one to five, a top priority with a value of five. Given the experienced facts from above, would you be calling this same company again if your furnace needed repaired? The answer is obviously no. Next week, you receive a customer satisfaction survey in the mail from the company, and they ask you: "On a scale of one to five, how would you rate your experience from our recent repair service?" Your response is a one, and I bet you have told all your friends about your experience. By the way, when you were telling them what happened, how much emotion did you place on the result (hot air blowing) versus the emotion you placed on the service not aligning with your expectations?

This example is one we have all shared and can all relate to. If your experience has not yet included furnace repair, how about auto repair or a home remodeling project? They all hold the same potential for the company's ideology toward customer service to generate positive or negative momentum toward future use of their service (customer satisfaction/loyalty). In this case, the multiple on results was 0.20. We can estimate the 0.20 value because the result had a priority of a five to the customer, but the customer's satisfaction was a one (five to the power of 0.20) even after the needed result was achieved. Want to see the power created when results and intent are aligning?

Okay, same set of facts. Only this time, at about 1:30 p.m., you get a call from the company informing you that the repair person has been required to spend longer on the job scheduled in front of yours. They expect the service tech to be at your house sometime between 3:00 p.m. and 3:30 p.m. They ask if you would still like to keep the service appointment at the new time, or would you like to reschedule for another day? You respond that you would like to keep the appointment. They end the conversation by assuring you that if the estimated arrival time changes, they will give you another call.

The same service tech arrives at the same time (3:15 p.m.). This time, you perceive his arrival as a positive, not a negative, simply because you have been given, in advance, the intent of the result. Your expectations have been re-established. You show the repair person the furnace, just as before. Only this time, as soon as they see your furnace, they explain to you that the unit is about twenty years old and that he may have the parts to fix it or he may not. He also says that it may very well cost about as much to fix the older unit as it would to replace it. You ask how much for a new unit, and the answer is somewhere between $5,500 and $6,000, depending on how much additional work will be needed to install the new unit. Then, you are asked if you want him to proceed with the repair. You don't have $6,000 to spend on a new furnace, so your hope is now for hot air blowing at a price well below the cost of a new unit. The repair person agrees to go ahead and find out what needs to be fixed, but they will tell you what they find and give you an idea on how much it will cost before they make the repair. You agree and walk away while he starts his work.

In about thirty minutes, he contacts you to let you know that he has located the problem and that he has the parts needed to fix it in the van. The parts are not inexpensive and will cost about $750. Also it will likely take another hour for him to install the parts. So, the total cost for the service call will be around $950. He then goes on to tell you that your furnace is in good shape for a twenty-year-old unit. With a unit that old, you never know what will go bad next, but this repair will get you up and running for now. You ask him if it was his furnace would he go ahead and spend the money for the repair. His response is: "Yes, but know that sometime in the not too distant future, you are going to need to replace the entire unit." You authorize him to complete the repair.

After picking up his tools, he returns from the service van with your bill, $975. Again, results equal hot air blowing. Environment is restored. Now, after this experience, how is your emotion of trust doing? Are you feeling the integrity? This time, I will bet your answers to both questions are decidedly positive. Why? There was a steady stream of substantive communication during the entire process. Each time, they established your expectations up front and respected your decision as to whether to proceed or not. Not only do you have the required change to your environment, but because their declared intent was offered at every decision point in the process, the impact on the actual result was a multiplying effect of greater than one.

Using the same assumptions as before, getting the hot air blowing again (the result) was, on a scale of priority one to five, a top priority with a value of five. Given the experienced facts from above, would you be calling this same company again if your furnace needed to be repaired or replaced? The answer is most likely, "yes." Next week, you receive a customer satisfaction survey in the mail from the company and they ask you: "On a scale of one to five, how would you rate your experience from our recent repair service?" Your response is a five, and I bet you have told several of your friends about your experience. When you were telling them what happened, how much emotion did you place on the result (hot air blowing) versus the emotion you placed on the service aligning with your expectations? In both the negative and the positive cases, the majority of the emotion shared with others will be focused on the alignment of the expectations with the results, not on the results themselves. Also, I can guarantee that you will go out of your way to bring up the negative experience in conversations, sharing the negative much more frequently than the positive. When given the opportunity, you will not hesitate to share a positive experience. Human nature is always fascinating. Next time, notice that when you share a negative experience with someone, you will receive empathy. However, when you share a positive experience, you will receive their attention.

In this case of a positive experience, let's estimate that the multiplying impact from intent was 2.00. The customer rated the needed result at the highest a priority, a five, the same as before. This time on the customer satisfaction survey, they chose the highest rating and took the time to write additional positive comments. The greatest value (5 to the power of 2.00 = 25) comes from the strengthening of the relationship and the positive influence being shared with the other members of the population. In the eyes of the customer and to the future growth of the repair company, the value of the opportunity began at a five. The actual results were the same in both cases. The alignment of result with intent drove the perceived value to a twenty-five. The lack of alignment drove the perceived value to a one.

Here is where this gets very interesting. The gaps between the value of the result (five) and the perceived future value of the result (one or twenty-five) represent the creation of momentum for change within the relationship. A five decreasing to a one represents the creation of negative momentum for future change (reduced trust, perceived lack of integrity, and no communication or meaningless communication).

A five increasing to a twenty-five represents the creation of positive momentum for future change, enhancing all of the internal elements and strengthening the relationship.

Positive momentum for change is created when the human need of purpose is aligned with the expectation of future value (intent). Negative momentum is created when the two factors do not align. Why is momentum so important to cultural transformation? The creation of momentum is actually the creation of capacity for change within an individual or a culture. Negative momentum serves to reduce the capacity for change. The creation of positive momentum serves to increase the capacity for change. Before moving on, let's use our furnace example one more time.

Answer this question for me: "Given the positive momentum created by the second example, results and intent being aligned, are you more or less likely to upgrade your furnace (change) in the future?" Answer: You are more likely to make the change because your expectations have been set for a similarly positive experience, the receipt of future value greater than just the installation of a new furnace. No one wants to spend $6,000 on a furnace, but faced with the *need*, would you choose to spend your money for an unknown future value or would you choose to invest your hard-earned money where you have an established set of value-added expectations? The answer is obvious, and this type of choice is one faced by the cultures gathered around the kitchen table every day.

Positive momentum for change is created when the human need of purpose is aligned with the expectation of future value.

Recall our definition of culture from Life Question #1:

"What is a culture? First, cultures exist everywhere. As the subtitle to this book would indicate, you will find cultures: '... From the Kitchen Table to the Boardroom and From Our Communities to Our Nation.' When two or more individuals

(a population) gather together, wherever that gathering may occur, you have the makings of a culture. Second, a culture is a population which shares a set of collective choices and needs. And finally, this set of cultural choices and needs is the product of interactions between three internal and three external cultural influences."

All of what we have learned so far regarding culture and cultural transformation is represented in this everyday example of a kitchen table culture. In this example of a furnace repair, the family culture has pulled together every aspect we have learned so far, from the Culture Model to the Cycle, from human *needs* and *choices* to the Core, and from the truth to the creation of momentum.

There is nothing particularly complicated about what has taken place within this example, once you learn to view the opportunity from a different perspective. Once you learn to hold it up to the light, you will see all of the colors (opportunities). You would be right if you are thinking: "This can't be this easy to understand? There has to be more to it." First, once you gain the perspectives offered in these three books, it will be shockingly easy for you to see the differing colors. What takes a while is the practice and learning from the experiences before you actually progress to a level of understanding. And, yes, there is more to learn regarding the cultural transformation process. For example: "What happens when ideology is applied to a larger population?" Answer: "The same as when it is applied at the kitchen table."

The Impact of Ideology on Culture:
Beyond the Kitchen Table

I happen to be writing this book during the winter. A few weeks ago, there was a massive cold front that impacted much of the eastern half of the United States. The term used by the meteorologists to describe this event was "polar vortex." Basically, what happens is that the winter cold normally occurring in the Arctic Circle shifts south, so cities like Chicago, for example, experienced wind-chill temperatures of minus forty degrees. These environmental conditions are deadly. I was in need of a clear example of extreme environmental or economic conditions in order to introduce the concept of ideology's impact on a larger population, and along came the polar vortex, giving me the example I needed.

What if you lived in the Arctic Circle? You, your family, your friends, and their families all lived in an environment where minus forty degrees during the winter was commonplace. Also, assume that this community had lived in this same environment for many generations. Given these environmental conditions, I would imagine that the focus of our hypothetical community would be on the human *needs* of safety and security. Safety and security form the culture's ideology in the way that leaders and culture characteristically prioritize development, select a course of action, and establish the perception of fact. Ideology will be focused on how to find shelter from the extreme cold and securing sources of food, water, and heat during the winter. I doubt the culture would place a high priority on actions or facts related to harvesting and properly preparing coconuts as a food source.

How would this necessary ideology impact the migration of Absent Facts and the Cycle of Human Development? The intent of this culture's ideology is to provide the population with the knowledge and the skills needed to achieve safety and security. The result of this ideology, aligning with the <u>intent</u> of the ideology, creates an accelerated, positive impact on the culture.

Illustration #9.a. below shows a concentration of Absent Facts migrating through the knowledge gap at an accelerated rate via a direct path created by ideology. Notice that some facts attempting to migrate from Absent to Present are rejected by the ideology giving priority to those facts which are perceived as acceptable. An example of fact being rejected by ideology may be harvesting and preparing coconuts. You can bet that the facts being accelerated into the Present are directly related to shelter, food, water, heat, etc.

Also, notice in the illustration the efficiency being created by ideology within the downstream segments from the gathering of facts to the formation of knowledge. There is no need and no time for multiple testing of data and information in order to create knowledge. At forty degrees

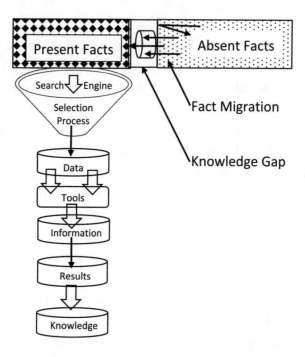

below zero, a member of the culture may die before going through all the normal learning loops. Think of it this way: In this environment, these are the declared set of actions or facts you need to know to be safe. Here is how you apply those facts, and this is why it is necessary for you to have this knowledge. This is a focused Cycle that is, direct and to the point, more efficient.

Keeping with our Arctic Circle example, the more effective and efficient the development Cycle, the more members of the population ultimately survive through the harsh winters. The increased number of surviving members share their experiences, and from the sharing of knowledge, the result is a population skilled at surviving the harsh winters. Given the ideological focus on shelter, food, water, and heat within the culture, they will progress before long from the *need* for safety to the *need* for security. This modified purpose for security will be embedded within the culture's ideology. Because security is so important, they will seek more than one path to ensure safety for the culture. The culture will be seeking multiple ways to survive in order to reduce the risk from a single point of failure. (Why risk the twenty-year-old furnace going out in the middle of next winter? Let's start saving money in order to replace it. It is the same process.)

Since we are dealing with a hypothetical, please allow me a little creative freedom in order to make my point. I realize the actual time frame for the example I am about to use would have been over several generations, but for our purposes, we are compressing the change process into a much shorter period of time. Assuming creative freedom, let's continue with our example. The population living in the Arctic Circle currently uses whale oil as their primary source for heat. What happens if their *need* for security leads them to consider other heat sources? Instead of only heating with whale oil, they choose to develop ways to heat with petroleum-based products, kerosene for example. After a few years of using kerosene for a heat source, their search for security evolved into heating with electricity produced by diesel powered generators. Each development, each learning loop within this progression, produces more effective and efficient methods of securing the population during the harsh winters. Before each new step, the leaders provided the population with a declared set of actions and facts. They provided a list of potential risks and rewards that may be encountered as the next innovation is put into place (spend $950 now to fix the furnace, and it may last for several years, or it may not).

As the transformation to kerosene took place, the actual results from the change aligned with the stated intent. When the leader was influencing the development of the culture to meet the *need* for security by improving sources of heat during the winter, he did so through a series of declared actions. The positive results from the leader's actions in switching the population to kerosene for heat were as intended; they aligned. Therefore, the leader's ideology was viewed by the population as providing future value greater than the results themselves. The multiplier effect of his intent was greater than the actual results, greater than one (1.00) because the stated intent was aligned with the results. Remember that: Ideology = Results to power of Intent. Under these circumstances, the leader may hear from the culture something like: "You told us you would improve our heating source, and you did it. Now, what about upgrading from kerosene to electricity? What does that look like? How do we take this next step?"

Result to the power of Intent (Ideology) is an important source of cultural momentum. Momentum (capacity) for transformation within a culture is increased when the intent is declared in advance and the actual results are aligned with the stated intent. This is true regardless of the impact on the culture. For example, what happens if the population demands that the leader change their heat source from kerosene back to the traditional whale oil? The same relationship applies. If the leader declares up front the negative impact of the change and the actual results are found to be aligned with the established expectations (declared intent), the leader's ideology is again viewed by the population as providing future value greater than the results themselves. Under these circumstances, the leader may hear from the culture something like: "You told us we wouldn't like the results of going back to using whale oil and you were right. Now, go ahead and take us from heating with whale oil to using electricity. You tell us what we need to do and we will make it happen. What benefits will electricity provide for us? How do we take this next step?"

> *Momentum (capacity) for transformation within a culture is increased when the intent is declared in advance and the actual results are aligned with the stated intent.*

Even though the actual results were not what the culture had hoped for, the negative expectations established by the leader resulted in successful application of ideology. "Results to the power of Intent" created the momentum needed for the next step in cultural development. Here is the downside. The creation of momentum for transformation within the culture typically places the leader's feet on the "treadmill of performance." This is the never-ending loop of expectations which is typically expressed as: "I know what you did last week, but what have you done for me lately?" Sound familiar? We need to explore two sides of this leadership trap. First, we need to explore: "What does it look like?" And second, we need to understand: "How can leaders avoid it?"

What does the treadmill of performance look like? Take a look at Illustration #9.b. below. This illustration shows us how the Cycle evolves to meet the new demands from the culture.

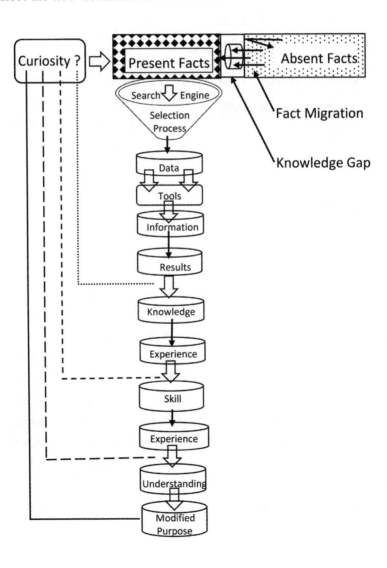

Notice that the efficiency of ideology has spread from its initial intent of attaining knowledge (quickly learning what you need to know in order to survive the winter cold) all the way through the Cycle. The same developmental focus (ideology) that accelerated the culture's ability to survive has now been extended downstream in the Cycle. The ideology now seeks to impose these new efficiencies on the development of skills, the scope of understanding and ultimately impacting purpose modification.

> *Ideology seeks to impose new efficiencies on the development of skills, the scope of understanding and ultimately impacts purpose modification.*

In this illustration, the leader has just begun to impose their ideology over the entire Cycle. They have either assumed the right to impose their intent over the culture's results or the leader was granted the right based on previous acceptable actions. Regardless of the root cause, the impact to cultural development is the same, restriction in order to accomplish the desired result.

Looking at the Cycle modeled in Illustration 9.b., please notice the reduction in the number of experiences shared after the knowledge is gained to accomplish the culture's goal. This is the developmental efficiency created by the successful application of ideology. Both the leader and the culture would respond the same way if questioned about the resulting lack of diversity in experience: "Why would we waste time exploring other options? We know what works. Keep going forward."

When we say that success breeds more success, the Cycle being modified in this manner causes this statement to become true. The external influence of expectations drives the culture to seek more and grander results faster. (The pace of the treadmill has now quickened, and the leader is no longer walking along the path. They are forced to run just to keep up with cultural demands.) In response, the leaders call for greater efficiencies in the developmental process and more influence (power) over the migration and selection of facts.

Please see Illustration #10 below. Continuing on with our example of heat sources in the Arctic Circle, Illustration #10 shows the changes to the Cycle implemented to accomplish the transformation of the culture to the next step in securing reliable sources of heat for the winter. This represents the path taken when changing from a kerosene-based heat source to electrical heat produced by diesel generators.

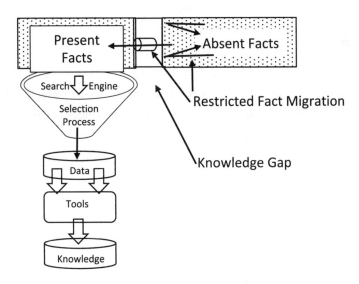

The first time we implemented change in order to meet the *need* of security, there was an acceleration of necessary Absent Facts into Present Facts. Some Absent Facts were restricted, but only because they didn't meet the population's immediate *need* for security. This time, in the interest of efficiency and to meet expectations, most Absent Facts are restricted and only those deemed necessary by the leader are permitted to migrate. Notice that the Universe of Present Facts, those facts that are discovered and accessible to the population via search engines, has now been restricted. (The background of the block representing the Universe of Present Facts has changed so that it now matches the background of the Absent Facts block.) Present Facts previously available to the population are now labeled as unnecessary in the pursuit of the goal. This too is an additional restriction on the population being put into place by the leader under the banner of efficiency.

To gain better control over the results, leadership has also reduced the steps in the Cycle. In our first application of ideology, the number of shared experiences were reduced in the interest of time and safety, but all of the steps were followed. Viewing this second round of transformation, we see that entire steps in the development process have been illuminated, all in the interest of meeting the demands of the population.

Because of the change from petroleum-based heating to the use of electric heat, we need to have people trained to perform maintenance on the generators. Others will be needed to install wiring. Still more members of the population need to drive trucks in order to haul the fuel to be stockpiled for the winter. Because the leader is running just to keep pace with cultural demand, there is no time for a long, drawn-out educational process. No, in the interest of efficiency and progress toward the established goal, the leaders will determine what knowledge is to be shared, and the people will need to do exactly as they are told.

I know you know where this is headed, and you are correct. But, allow me one more layer of ideological development. The community now has the diesel generators in place. Members of the population have been taught to maintain the generators, fuel the generators, and run additional wiring to distribute the electricity from the generators to even more buildings in the community, etc. Once again, the leaders of the population have declared their intent and they have delivered the results. Results and intent are aligned and the momentum (capacity) for change is even greater now that the population has seen the successful implementation of two major changes. Logic would dictate if this way of leadership worked for heat, why not take the same approach to solving some of our other problems: building roads, educating children, or providing health care?

Hearing these new requests from the population, the leader will be likely to say to himself: "I was right with my approach to solving the heat problems for my people. They will be more than happy when I use the same ideology in my approach to providing for their health care." Or, the more likely scenario, the population literally demands of the leader: "You fixed our problem with finding a reliable source of heat during the winter, now do the same thing and provide for our health care needs. You lead, we'll follow." The leader is now running uphill on the treadmill of performance.

At the same time, word of this culture's success has spread to other cultures in the region. They too are in need of safety and security. In an effort to help their fellow man, the culture and the leader reach out to these other communities to show them how to establish a reliable source of heat, accomplishing security. Which model of the Cycle do you think they will share with these new groups: the original model with multiple, shared experiences or the more efficient model with restricted access to facts and missing steps in the development process? Of course, they will implement the latter, not because they want to control the downstream cultures, but they know this is what worked for them. They assume it will work best for the new group. After all, there really isn't enough time to consider going through a drawn-out educational process. We need to get these other cultures fixed, then move forward and fix our health care system!

Lost in the effort to replicate success, to keep running faster, is the "why" behind the success. In the interest of efficiency, everyone focuses on "what" changed and "how" the change was implemented. In the place of "why" stands ideology. Growing exponentially with every success, ideology fills the gaps in development created by unknown facts, unshared experiences, and deleted steps in human development. Intent is no longer declared up front. There is no multiplying effect from intent being aligned with results; therefore, there is little to no momentum for change created within the population. The formula for Ideology is unchanged: Ideology = Results to the power of Intent. The results (the truth) are still the results. It is the power of the Intent factor which has changed. As ideology fills in more and more of the deleted pieces from the Cycle, the multiplying effect of Intent is reduced to a value of less than one (1.00).

Let's state this another way. (Right back to the Kitchen Table example, they are one in the same.) If Results are assigned an expectation value of five by the culture and Intent, being declared in advance and aligned with results is a two, the future value of the ideology is twenty-five (5 x 5 or 5 to the power of 2). In this equation, all facts are discoverable by the population, and all experiences are shared. The Cycle remains intact, and the expected future value of the leadership's ideology is much greater than the current value of the results (twenty-five is greater than five). This method of applying ideology is less efficient but creates capacity for future change. This is short-term pain in exchange for long-term gain.

> *In the interest of efficiency, everyone focuses on "what" changed and "how" the change was implemented. In the place of "why" stands ideology.*

If Results are assigned the same expectation value of five by the culture and Intent is a value of 0.2, because intent was not declared in advance so its alignment with results will be an unknown, the future value of the ideology is one. In this equation, not all facts are discoverable by the population and only those experiences deemed as necessary by the leader are shared. In this case, the Cycle has been restricted for the sake of efficiency. The expected future value of the leadership's ideology is much less than the current value of the results. This method of applying ideology is more efficient but creates no capacity for future change. This is short-term gain in exchange for long-term pain.

These two values are just arbitrary numbers, designed to be polar opposites, for illustration purposes. The first example illustrates a home run for the leader and the culture. Massive amounts of momentum (capacity) for future change would be created along with the granting of additional trust and integrity from the population to the leader.

Additional trust and integrity have been granted based on the substantive communication of intent, which aligned with results, create greater influence. Because there were no restrictions on the Cycle during the transformation process, the population is in a position to better understand future communications of intent from the leader. You have heard the phrase: "They have built a culture of success." This is how it is constructed. Ideology = Results to the power of Intent where Intent is greater than one (1.00). In this example, the multiplying effect is much greater than 1.00. This is an illustration of the Transformational Leadership Model, which we will explore in our next and final section: "Life Question #6: How do you transform a culture?"

The second example, changing to the new heat source, illustrates the accomplishment of the same result but in a completely different way. The task was completed. Check the box, or cross that one off the list. The leader has delivered, and the culture has received but at what cost? Notice there is no perception of greater future value on the part of the culture. Therefore, there was no momentum for future change created. Why? Because the leader drastically restricted the population's access to facts, information, and knowledge (the Cycle) in order to gain efficiency within the change process. The leader leveraged and consumed existing levels of granted trust and integrity, while choosing not to communicate intent. The population moved forward with little to no understanding of the process and no increase in their ability to anticipate the leader's future actions (a reduction in trust). This is the classic example of when the leader will say: "Just do what I say, when I say, and how I say and I will get us there." Ideology = Results to the power of Intent where Intent is less than one (1.00). In this example, the multiplying effect of Intent is a reduction to momentum (capacity) where the impact of the Ideology applied equates to less than the Result itself. This is an illustration of the Terminal Leadership process.

Now, step back and look at the big picture. Are you more likely to remain as the leader if your ideology has a perceived future value of twenty-five or one? The answer is obvious, twenty-five. If you scored a one, you have two courses of action available to you, assuming you wish to remain in a position of leadership. Learn to lead differently or attempt to change the equation. Since this entire series of books is about showing you "why" and "how" to lead differently, we'll focus on exploring the leader's second option: changing the Ideology equation.

In order for a leader to effectively change the Ideology equation, they must make the *choice* of arrogance over humility. Once the internal *choice* of arrogance is made, the rest of the changes are easily justified. The conversation the leader may have with himself goes something like this. *"After all, these people I am leading are ignorant of the facts. They don't understand the complexity of the changes necessary in order for me to deliver what they said they want?* (Note: the population's lack of understanding and not knowing the facts is a function of the leader's own actions, restricting the Cycle in order to implement change more efficiently. This is always a self-fulling prophecy.) *If they only knew the challenges I face on a daily basis in order to take care of them, they would appreciate what I am doing."* The irony is unmistakable.

The leader continues: *"The real problem here is not the results; they got what they wanted. The real problem is that these people don't understand. They don't appreciate how hard it is to implement these changes. They should be grateful that I am working so hard on their behalf. They need to learn to appreciate my intent, regardless of the outcome. When I switched them from heating with whale oil to using kerosene, they didn't really appreciate what I did for them. I even helped them to switch back to whale oil for a little while. I told them it wouldn't work. They eventually learned what I was trying to tell them all along; electric heat was the way to go. Now that I changed them to electric heat, they want me to help other communities to make the change to electricity, and as if that isn't enough, they want me to take on improving their health care system. There is no way that I can get all of this stuff they want done without more control. I need more control so I can make the process of change more efficient. More control, that's the only way I can get them what they want. What they are wanting me to accomplish is very difficult, and whether I get it done or not, they had better appreciate my effort."*

Can you hear this conversation actually taking place? Maybe you have had a similar conversation in your own mind as your leadership responsibilities grew. I know I did, many years ago, when my responsibilities changed from working *for* people to working *with* them. This conversation and my reaffirmation of my *choice* of humility is what drove the creation of Leadership Rule #1 and the critical role played by respect in the leadership process. I approach the responsibilities of leadership knowing that I am never in possession of all the facts. I understand that it is impossible for me to know all that is needed to be known. But, I have learned that scattered among those around me are the facts I need. All I had to do was develop the skills necessary to work with others in order to help create opportunities for growth.

In the leader's conversation above, did you hear the migration of ideology from one of being results-based to the less risky intent-based? This is what I meant earlier when I referenced change the equation. As the challenges of leadership become increasingly more complex (often overwhelming), it is common for leaders to distance themselves from the risk of failure by minimizing the actual result and focusing the culture on the importance of their original intent. This shift in perception allows the leader's ideology to be

> *It is common for leaders to distance themselves from the risk of failure by minimizing the actual result and focusing the culture on the importance of their original intent.*

viewed as successful, maintaining a perceived future value to the culture which is greater than the actual result. To accomplish this perception, the culture needs to be taught to accept intent as having a future value equal to that of actual results. Taking this shift in cultural perception out to its ultimate conclusion, acceptable intent can create momentum for change regardless of the actual results. We now have two very different equations for cultural ideology.

The first expression of ideology is the traditional equation: Ideology = Results to the power of Intent. These are the cultures led by the shared knowledge gained from actual results. The second equation is: Ideology = acceptable intent. These are the cultures led by the perception of acceptable intent. We now have established the classic contrast in cultural development. Both cultures are based on the same sets of external and internal influences, but they differ in their ideologies.

> *Two very different equations for cultural ideology:*
> *Ideology = Results to the power of Intent; and*
> *Ideology = acceptable intent*

Creating momentum (capacity) for change within the culture of the Haves is result-based, where knowledge powers the transformation. Possessing knowledge is power. The members of this culture "have" knowledge, which powers their transformation, forming the foundations of freedom and independent development. Capitalism.

Creating momentum (capacity) for change within the culture of the Have-nots is intent-based, where perception powers the transformation. Possessing knowledge is still power, but its possession is tightly controlled. The members of the Have-nots culture have knowledge but it is primarily formed from the perception of acceptable intent. The transformation of this culture will be one of broader and tighter restrictions over cultural freedom and independent development. Socialism.

Think back to <u>A Transformational Conversation</u> at the beginning of this book. When I spoke with the MB team for the first time, my approach was results-based to the extreme. Everything we did during the meeting was to reinforce a culture of transparency and unrestricted access to knowledge, except for knowledge prohibited by federal regulation. They knew those were the only restrictions on the future migration of Absent Facts. My first direct action taken as the group's leader was to reduce their fear of failure by personally assuming the responsibility for everything that went wrong. Next, I established a second "Result to the power of Intent" scenario by stating that they would be given the credit for everything that went right as a result of the RB/MB acquisition. Stop and think about the three critical actions that were taken that evening: total transparency, reduced fear of failure, and the promise of future reward and recognition for accomplishments. Given what you now know about cultural transformation, do you see what I did and why?

My sole purpose for that meeting was to start building momentum (capacity) for change within the RB/MB employee culture. Step one was to establish a short-term set of expectations in order to develop a new ideology. I began by declaring, in advance, a set of intentions and defining the results. Example: Part of RB's culture is transparency (establish the intent). Here is everything we know regarding the acquisition up to this point. These are the people you can contact to get even more information as it becomes available, and this is how you can contact them. This example shows the delivery of the actual result. The stated intent of transparency and the result of transparency were aligned. The fact

> *As a leader, you can't accomplish change on your own, so why pretend that you can?*

that the intent and result were delivered within minutes of each other is irrelevant. Momentum for change was created. Momentum, the capacity of others to participate in accomplishing change, is the answer to: "How can leaders avoid stepping on the treadmill of performance?" As a leader, you can't accomplish change on your own, so why pretend that you can?

I continued by building on the transparency theme, taking personal ownership of all that was going to go wrong in the acquisition process.

Crazy, right? Wrong. I was establishing an expectation that was perceived as a huge risk by everyone in the room, including Anna. In fact, given my personal character, I was already holding myself directly accountable for everything that would go wrong, no matter who was at fault. My declaration of intent to accept all of the risk was nothing more than a re-statement of an existing result. By declaring it publicly, I created an additional expectation within the population. Each time they saw the actual result take place, and there were many, additional momentum for change was created. Again, expectations were established and then met within a few minutes of each other, building even greater momentum.

The same logic applies to my stated intent of giving them all the credit for whatever went right. This was nothing more than a reflection of Leadership Rule #1 (respect for yourself and everyone around you) and my personal *choice* of humility. I never accept credit for positive results. It makes me very uncomfortable. I will always pass the credit on to others who deserve it much more than me. Setting this expectation for the MB group and then delivering on established intent was natural for me, and it generated the added benefit of creating more momentum for change within the culture.

Remember when I said that I knew this first meeting was a success because the vast majority of the post-meeting questions were for Anna and Jill, focusing on the future? Now you know "why" I knew that was indeed the case. The ideology put forward, Results in alignment with Intent, created a perception of future value greater than the actual results. I don't think we scored a "twenty-five" but we did accomplish something much greater that a "five." And, please note that momentum was created within a ninety-minute meeting at minimal financial cost to RB's Core.

The MB group was emerging from a restrictive but financially successful culture into a less successful but more Core-driven transformative culture. Everything I could have done that evening to allow them to experience, prove, or believe the facts I was presenting served to strengthen their capacity for change.

During our conversation on the way home that evening, Anna was right when she commented on the risk I was taking. Eventually, that risk would catch up with me, and I would pay a price for being the catalyst for change (leading the transformation process). However, during the next two or three years, all members of the RB Core were the beneficiaries of cultural transformation. My family did well, and new opportunities for our growth kept presenting themselves. When it was time for me to pay the price, the pain was short-lived and the gain was life-altering. So much of success in life depends on your perspective. I always recommend that you choose to LIVE better by understanding how to LEAD differently.

The final piece of our journey through the cultural transformation process is understanding the Transformational Leadership Model itself. Once we understand Transformational Leadership, we will be ready to explore the processes involved in leading purposeful change. Change management or, more appropriately, change leadership is the subject of Book 3: change to LIVE better & LEAD differently.

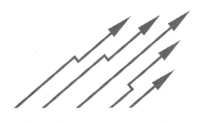

Life Question #6
HOW DO YOU
TRANSFORM A CULTURE?

We are now ready to assemble all that we have covered in Book 2 and answer the question of how cultural transformation is actually accomplished. You already know the basic answer, which is cultures are transformed by leadership/influence. Surprise, surprise! Where do we start? We begin at the foundation for all leadership. We start with understanding.

First, there is no magic wand for changing a culture. Whether it is large or small, impacting a culture is easily done. External and internal influences are constantly adjusting cultural norms and perspectives. Cultural change is occurring every minute of every day. Many leaders will tell you that much of their time is spent in an effort to maintain the current culture, or to counteract the external and internal forces of change. Whether the intent is to transform or to maintain a culture, the leader contributes to the change process with each word and each action taken or not taken. Leadership, in all of its forms, generates the substance being communicated to the population.

> *Cultural change is occurring every minute of every day.*

We know from the Culture Model that there are three external influences constantly at work producing change. Economic and environmental conditions continuously shift, and cultural expectations are always evolving. Remember our example of global weather patterns and our developing ability to predict hurricanes? We have learned that even the most complex external influences can become predictable when you have the needed information and the right models.

We also know from the Culture Model that there are three internal influences producing cultural change. The internal influences are trust, integrity, and communication. Feeding the internal influences are the catalysts of emotion, purpose, and substance. The catalysts circulate within the collective relationship much like our blood circulates within our bodies.

Now that we have had a quick review, let's begin our exploration of cultural transformation by stating the obvious; there is a huge difference between changing a culture and transforming a culture. It is comparable to the difference between random change (cause and effect) and purposeful change, which is accomplished when results align with intent. One just happens and the other takes meaningful effort, understanding, and skill.

Leading cultural change is the ability to react to the effects caused by internal and external influences. Leading this level of cultural change is most effective when it is efficient. Remember our example of changing the sources of heat for the population living in the Arctic Circle? The more restricted the Cycle, the more efficient the change. When focused on efficiency, the leader learns enough to identify the cultural influences in play, decides on the course of action, and implements the change. In the presence of leadership founded on efficiency, the contribution from the members of the culture boils down to: "do as you are told." Under efficient leadership, your job is to execute the assigned tasks when you are told and how you are told. If your leadership style is creating the "do as you are told" environment, welcome to the treadmill of performance. Every day, the leadership treadmill will roll faster and faster as the leader places an increasing priority on efficiency.

Transforming a culture contains the same elements as cultural change; however, a leader attempting to transform a culture will prioritize the elements differently. Understanding still remains at the foundation of the transformational approach to cultural change. It just requires a much greater allocation of the leader's time and effort. Remember the time I spent up front in order to understand the MB acquisition? All of the time spent to understand MB, from multiple perspectives, was done in anticipation of the opportunity to create momentum (capacity for change) within the MB team during that first meeting. How about the amount of time spent in the creation of the Model for Balanced Change? Why invest all of the time and effort, up front, in order to create an instructional aid? Answer: The model enabled me to effectively illustrate the leadership challenges created for the Culture by changes in the perceptions of the customer and shareholder groups. The driving force behind the time invested in the creation of these models, teaching tools, and even the creation of this series of books is all tied to creating the capacity (momentum) for transformation. The first priority is to influence your own personal transformation, then you can turn your attention to influencing the transformation of the cultures around you. First learn to understand, and then, take the time to teach.

When I say that my reason for writing these books is to give back, and to help others live better and lead differently, I am really attempting to help you to change your current perspective. The goal is for you

> *The first priority is to influence your own personal transformation, learn to understand, and then, take the time to teach.*

to hold life up to the light so you can see all of the opportunities for learning and to better understand how to create capacity for change within yourself and others. That is the best way I can summarize my spending what will turn out to be the better part of three years writing these books. My goals are to help you understand your potential; generate the results needed to accomplish your purpose; and to learn the necessary skills so you can teach others the "how" and the "why" behind living better and leading differently.

The first words written in Book 1 were: "First Understand and Then Teach." Are you beginning to see what these words mean to me and why I began this journey by sharing them with you? First understand. Understanding is the foundation of all learning and, therefore, all leadership. Pictures are worth thousands of words. Let's use a few pictures, along with a few words, to transfer the concept of cultural transformation based on the foundation of understanding. After a few pages of illustrations used to lay out the Transformational Leadership process, we are going to return to that first meeting with the MB team. This time, the flap on the tent will be held wide open for you to view inside using a new perspective.

Please see Illustration #11.a below. This is a side by side comparison of Book 1's Communication Model (on the left) and the newly introduced Learning Model (on the right). Much like our earlier use of the Relationship Model from Book 1 as the foundation for the more inclusive Culture Model, these two models build on each other. Just as we begin by learning at one level, "Hot! Don't touch!" our level of understanding increases as we progress along the Cycle. The more one understands, the greater their capacity (momentum) for learning. These illustrations are just the next step toward an increased level of understanding.

> *The more one understands, the greater their capacity (momentum) for learning.*

Notice how the three elements of each model are the same. In both models, Information and Knowledge form the point of perception on which Substance and Communication are balanced, all being supported by a foundation of Understanding. The infrastructure of the models differs, but they are completely interdependent. From Book 1, we know that Filtration, Selection, and Listening are the three elements resulting in substantive

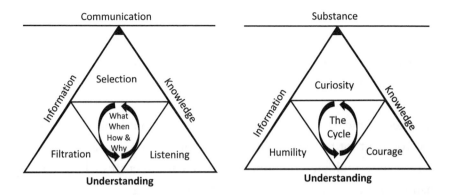

Communication. In constant circulation among the elements, keeping them strong, are the catalyst questions of: "What, When, How, and Why?" We don't need to include the "who" because we already know who "They" are. "They" are the parties influenced by the relationship.

Forming the internal structure of the Learning Model are the human *choices* of Humility, Curiosity, and Courage. In circulation among the *choices*, keeping them constantly renewed, we find the Cycle of Human Development. These three *choices* work together with the Cycle to create the learning loops, which result in Substance (needed and necessary communication) being delivered.

We could build many combinations to demonstrate the interdependence between these two models, but in the interest of time, let me give you just a few examples. Without the daily *choice* of Humility, I would not care enough about you to take into account your Filtration system when preparing a presentation. Without Humility, I would simply select words and examples that held meaning to me. During the ride back to RB's offices after the MB meeting, do you recall Anna commenting on the risks I took by not delivering the standard presentation for those types of meetings? My prioritizing the choice of delivering substance over deferring personal risk would not have been possible without my placing their needs above my own. In order for the risk to pay off by generating benefit for the RB Core, I had to put my presentation into terms that would register with the audience (be granted passage through their individual Filtration systems). I chose to assume an elevated level of short-term risk for the opportunity to create momentum, a long-term gain. It was a classic example of working smarter. There will be more on how this all works together in the next section.

My choosing to be Curious regarding the audience's needs is necessary in order for me to search for the Selection of an appropriate presentation environment for the group. The selection of an appropriate environment can include multiple components. The environment can be a combination of: the location of the meeting, the arrangement of the room, the location of the presenter, the visual and instructional aids used, the non-verbals, etc. I chose to deliver our first MB presentation in a location that was convenient to the audience, but most importantly, the environment established a stark contrast to their previous culture. The MB environment they were accustomed to was big city, big buildings, and high-tech. I could have chosen to compete with the familiar MB environment by having the meeting held in RB's newly renovated training center. That choice would have sent a clear message to the group. If I chose to compete with MB, the message delivered by the competing environment would have been: "RB's culture is more of the same, just on a smaller scale." Instead, I chose to contrast the environments, leading to a message of different, maybe better, and certainly, there is hope for the future.

Understanding Transformational Leadership will take Courage for me to Listen to the feedback from the audience during and after the presentation. Every piece of feedback I receive from the MB audience, verbal and nonverbal, generates another learning loop within the Cycle, leading me to a greater understanding of What, When, How, and Why. Do you see how and why these two models are completely interdependent? Think back to the meeting with the MB team. Now, consider the understanding you currently possess versus what you understood when you first read the story. Your growth is a product of the Communication Model and the Learning Model working together to enhance your leadership foundation. You now have an increased level of understanding, and you are gaining a different perspective.

Knowing that the foundation for Transformational Leadership is understanding, it follows that the greater the leadership challenge, the greater the need for understanding. I am going to ask you to expand your understanding of how and why all these models work together. When I introduced the Culture Model, I asked you to visualize the model as a globe, a three-dimensional model. We need to visualize understanding as the base of the four-sided pyramid. The foundation for all leadership is understanding. Please see Illustration #11.b. below. It illustrates the combination of the Communication and Learning Models. This structure resides at the foundation for all leadership. The size of the foundation shrinks or expands as the leadership type changes. The largest foundation is required to support Transformational Leadership. Varying amounts of understanding are required to support the many levels of Transitional Leadership. The traditional application of Terminal Leadership requires almost no foundation of understanding.

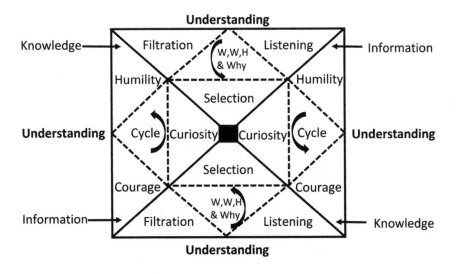

When you look at Illustration #11.b, notice the logic of the pairings. Let's start with the support structure closest to the foundation of understanding. If you are going to acquire information, you need to be humble and have the courage to listen, really listen. To filter the communication so that it contains substance for your audience, you need to have the humility and courage to put their needs ahead of your own.

The human *choice* of curiosity and the power of selection form the top of the pyramid. They are the most acceptable methods of transferring knowledge, which continuously drives substance and communication forward. And, at the heart of all of these functions, in constant motion tending to the needs of the entire support system, you will find the Cycle. The Cycle will provide new learning opportunities while working in concert with the power of asking better questions (What, When, How, and Why). All of these pairings serve to enhance understanding, supporting the foundation of leadership.

> *You need to have the humility and courage to put their needs ahead of your own.*

Illustration #11.b may, at first glance, appear to be a little complex, but isn't that a reflection of leadership's true nature? The good news is you now understand "how" the foundational pieces fit together and "why" they function so well together. The next, and final, layer of the combined Learning and Communication Models is balancing the results on the points of perception formed by Information and Knowledge. The two results are Substance from the Learning Model and meaningful Communication from the Communication Model. Please see Illustration #11.c below.

Balancing the results from the combined models prohibits us from using a teeter-totter approach. Maintaining balanced communication is more akin to balancing a round table top (the shaded area) on a single support post (the black square in the center formed by the combined points of perception). The wider the center support surface, the more stable the communication.

Here is a key point. The more commonly known the shared experiences are among the population, the larger the surface for supporting

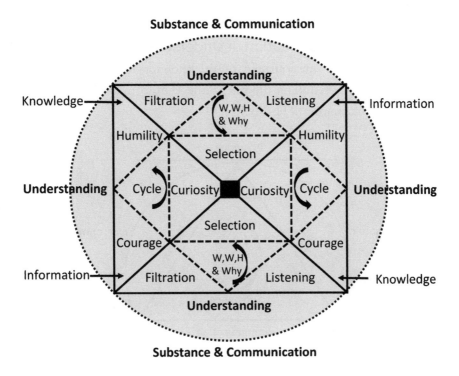

substance and communication. Said another way, when results align with intent and the understanding of purpose is shared by all, additional capacity to support the transformational process is created. Balance is maintained as the result of a collective effort, less dependent on a single leader's ability to keep running uphill on the treadmill of perfor-

> *The creation of common points of perception is the power of momentum*

mance. The creation of common points of perception is the power of momentum (additional capacity for cultural change) generated by the use of Transformational Leadership.

Let's continue to build on the foundation formed by understanding.

Cultural Transformation:
Building on the Foundation of Understanding

The next steps in our journey toward knowing how to transform a culture involves assembling the rest of the Transformational Leadership Model. See Illustration #11.d below.

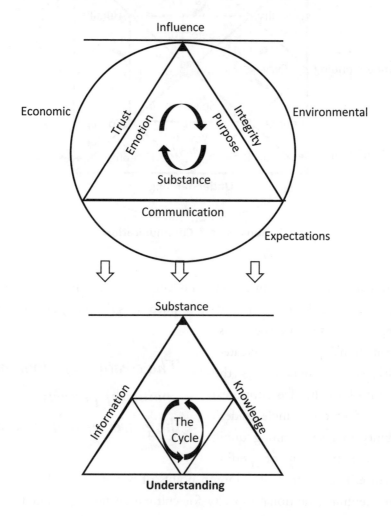

We are now ready to combine the Culture Model with the Learning Model. The Learning Model is shown in a simplified, two–dimensional form. This was done for purposes of illustration only. Notice that in Illustration #11.d overlaps exist after the combination of the two models.

The areas of overlap act like connecting plates with pre-drilled holes enabling us to bolt the models together. The result of Substance from the Learning Model connects to the catalyst of Substance in the Culture Model. The Learning Model's result of Communication matches up with the foundation of Communication from the Culture Model. The Culture Model's Expectations overlap the common points of perception, shared Curiosity, and Selection within the Learning Model. Once bolted together, the two models function as a single process. After they are assembled, the Culture Model's result of Influence is supported by Substance and Communication, with Understanding from the Learning Model serving as a foundation for the entire process.

The time has come for us to complete the construction of the Transformational Leadership Model. See Illustration #11.e below. We are bolting together the result of Influence with the Core's foundation of Culture. This is a solid connection point which runs the entire length of the overlap. After all, who are we influencing during the transformational process? The Culture. Influence and Culture are hand in glove, a perfect fit.

The Transformational Leadership Model is now completely assembled. See Illustration #11.f below.

Let's briefly review how we assembled the Transformational Leadership Model. The ultimate **Results** from transformation are balanced on the perceptions of the customers and the shareholders, which are supported by the Culture. Influence on the Culture is balanced on the Culture's perceptions of Trust and Integrity, as well as perceived Economic and Environmental Conditions. These Cultural perceptions are maintained by the catalysts of Emotion, Purpose, and Substance. All of the Expectations and catalysts, working together to produce Influence on the Culture, are supported by Substance and Communication. Substance and Communication are balanced on the point of perception formed by Information and Knowledge obtained through the application of human *choice* and the elements of communication. These applications are all nurtured and grown by the Cycle of Human Development.

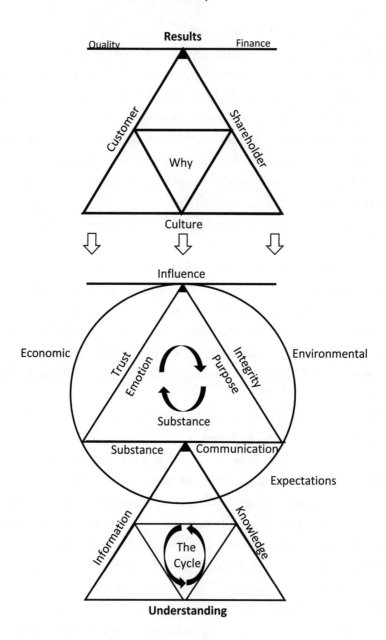

And supporting it all, every element, choice, catalyst, learning loop, and **Result** is a foundation built on **Understanding**.

Would you like to see the teaching equation for Transformational Leadership? Here you go: Transformational Leadership = Results to

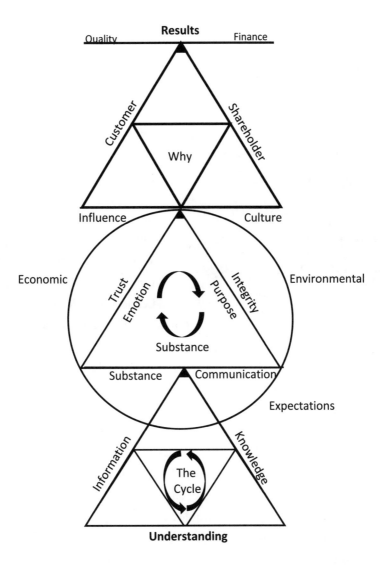

the power of Understanding. How is this different from the momentum created by Ideology? Ideology = Results to the power of Intent. Momentum generated by Results to the power of Intent is really based on the leader's ability or willingness to communicate Intent. Therefore, momentum created by Ideology is dependent on the skill, strength, and stamina of the leader. (How long can they run uphill on the treadmill of performance?)

Momentum created by the power of Understanding is based on the entire Culture's ability and willingness to focus on a shared purpose. Therefore, the momentum created by Understanding is dependent on the development process itself (the Cycle). Momentum generated from Understanding is not limited to the capacity of a single leader or even a selected few. Momentum born of Understanding possesses the stamina of many and an unlimited capacity to effect change. Why? In a word, perspective. Under the Transformational Leadership Model, change, held to the light, is perceived as opportunity. The opportunities to succeed or fail are seen as equals, and both are welcomed as yet another chance to learn. This is why I always encourage leaders to never stop learning! What I am really saying is: "Never miss out on the opportunity to understand the results."

> *Momentum born of Understanding possesses the stamina of many and an unlimited capacity to effect change.*

Cultural Transformation: Pulling back the flap on the tent.

During our journey through Book 2, I have asked you to join me as we constructed models, used teaching equations to help illustrate human nature, and cited numerous examples as to "how" and "why" leading differently matters. Now that we have covered the necessary concepts, it is time to pull this material together in a way that will make what you have learned more real.

The best way I know to do this is to revisit *A Transformational Conversation* from the first section of the book. Only this time, you will be viewing it with a fresh set of eyes, a new perspective. It is a perspective geared toward learning to lead cultural transformation, not the standard leadership approach where you strive to accomplish a list of tasks as quickly as possible. You want to step off of the treadmill of performance and help others to do the same? Make the commitment, as a leader, to understand and generate momentum, and then, teach others so they can help you to transform the culture you share. If you take the transformational approach to leadership, those around you will be helping you while, at the same time, they are helping themselves. How? We go back to the beginning with *A Transformational Conversation* **v. 2.0.**

Just a quick note. I have edited the original story so **v. 2.0** includes only the most relevant events from the presentation that evening. Gone is Jill's backstory. I have also removed

> *If you take the transformational approach to leadership, those around you will be helping you while they are helping themselves.*

most of the descriptive language regarding our ride back to the office after the meeting. The focus of **v. 2.0** is to show you how to begin the process of stepping off of the performance treadmill and to point out that there is always more to be learned from the experience. You just need to hold it up to the light.

From this re-telling of the meeting with the MB employees, I hope to pass along more benefit from my experiences. I want you to benefit not only from additional insights into what happened before and during the meeting but also to learn from a few peeks into the future to see how those events, which began in one ninety-minute meeting, impacted my Kitchen Table, Boardroom, and Community cultures. Any new content within the story has been underlined so it will stand out as you revisit the example. Back to the beginning.

It was around 5:30 in the afternoon when we pulled into the parking lot. My memory of exact dates from twenty-some years ago is a little sketchy, but my recollection regarding the impact from this event is crystal clear. I was driving a white Ford Taurus sedan with a gray cloth interior. It still had that new car smell. This was a company car provided for my use by RB.

I was RB's controller, and I was the merger and acquisition ("M&A") guy. Actually, I wore a bunch of different responsibility hats during the typical workday, as did most of the executive team at RB. I was just like many of you. I was burning the candle at both ends and had been for years. My feet had been firmly affixed to the treadmill of performance, but I was at the beginning stages of teaching myself how to step off the never-ending, uphill climb. Up to this point, the more my leadership skills grew, the more ways I was being pulled to help others. I had been a student of leadership, business, total quality management, reengineering, strategic planning, human nature, and communication since the age of nineteen (my first leadership role). At about thirty-six, I had learned, mostly through the school of hard knocks, how to help businesses and people to grow. I had learned to spot God-given talents in others and how to reach out, helping them to see their own potential. Building a business was fun, but my passion is helping people to grow.

I was a husband and the father of a pre-schooler. I served RB as controller for the bank; controller for the holding company; an executive member on numerous regulatory and investment committees; and primary M&A leader (every aspect of M&A from prospecting, to negotiation, to integration, and all steps in-between). I was also RB's conversion specialist; strategic planning team member; a leadership mentor; and about a half-dozen other lesser functions. In addition to my responsibilities at home and at the office, I had been an adjunct college professor for several years, where I taught one or two nights a week, and I volunteered in our community. That is nothing beyond what most of you do on a day-to-day basis. My purpose in making this partial list of responsibilities is to let you know that if I found a way to step off the treadmill, I can help you find your way off as well.

Everything begins with understanding, which includes learning how to step off the treadmill of performance. First understand the models, concepts, and influences at work within all collective relationships (the purpose of Book 2). Once you have the foundation in place, begin to teach yourself to perceive your leadership responsibilities as residing within different cultures. Separate them out into different buckets so they will be easier to carry. Husband, father, son, brother, and family is the culture you encounter at the Kitchen Table. Next, identify which responsibilities are contained within the boardroom (the job-related) bucket. Community cultural responsibilities are self-explanatory; they are those that impact the communities in which you live. And, finally, a few will have responsibilities that impact our nation. I will address that particular cultural bucket in the last section of the book titled *Cultural Transformation: One Nation; Two Cultures; Three Generations.*

Now, ask yourself which of these cultural groupings require your physical and emotional presence? Set your ego aside when answering this question. The need to be all things to all people is what started the treadmill running in the first place. Here is how I approached slowing the treadmill so I could eventually step off. The same approach will work for you. I started by asking: "Can I teach someone else to assume my responsibilities at the Kitchen Table?" No. That cultural transformation process absolutely requires my participation. Notice I said "participation." I did not use the word "presence." Whenever you decide that cultural transformation actually requires you, then you are all in. Just being present doesn't transform anyone.

How about the boardroom? This one is a mixed bag. Here is how I approach every company I walk into, regardless of the executive position I hold. Liter-

> *Literally from day one, I begin searching for someone internally or recruit someone from the outside to be my replacement.*

ally from day one, I begin searching for someone internally or recruit someone from the outside to be my replacement. And, once I understand the various responsibilities of others, then I prompt them to begin searching for and educating their replacement. Every task, every responsibility that doesn't absolutely require "me" can be and should become someone else's responsibility. I have never been in a situation where I failed to find someone more talented than I to assume the assignable responsibilities. In RB's boardroom culture, I was already in the process of educating my replacement for controller. I was stepping off of various committees, making room for others to grow through the experience, and Jill was on track to assume the lead role in the conversion process. Those areas that required my personal participation (M&A, strategic planning, and mentoring) remained with me until I could find someone who was better for the RB Core than me. None of this happens if you have not chosen humility; leave your ego out of this process.

The Community bucket was approached in the same way. I either had time to teach college classes, which I very much enjoyed, or I didn't. When I stepped away from that responsibility, it was because I no longer had the capacity to participate at the level I required of myself. I also had found an excellent person to take my place at the front of the class. Know your limits and know your priorities. Your ego is not the one working six or seven days a week. Leadership Rule #3: Maintain balance in life, have fun! Rule #3 isn't just a nice thing to do when you find the time. It is an absolute necessity for yourself and for those you lead. Without Rule #3, you are doomed to stay on the treadmill.

> *Leadership Rule #3:*
> *Maintain balance*
> *in life, have fun!*

We were a regional bank holding company located in southeastern Ohio. Our roots in the region were deep and went back over a hundred years. During the first ninety plus years of the bank's existence, we had grown to around $500 million in assets. We were not large enough to be big but big enough to start buying up some of the smaller community banks in the area.

On this day, our M&A activity had brought myself and two other trusted members of the RB team to a small, rural community in southeastern Ohio. "Trusted" means they were in the process of assuming some of my responsibilities. When you are seeking to replace yourself, you most likely will find several people that can help you with carrying the different buckets. Choose only those individuals with whom you can build a productive relationship. The town was located on the Ohio side of the Ohio River and was connected to the state of West Virginia with a narrow, two-lane bridge. As you already know, most everything about this transaction (as with most M&A transactions) carries a dual meaning and so it was with the location of these branches. RB had several locations along the Ohio River, directly across from West Virginia. We had been working with the state of West Virginia for some time, seeking permission to branch into their state, and we had been denied. This acquisition not only expanded our strategic footprint within attractive markets in our home state of Ohio, but it gave us even more justification for being granted permission to serve a broader segment of the West Virginia market. The strategy eventually worked in RB's favor. As with most downtown parking lots in this part of the country, the lot had been constructed over the vacant ground where a thriving downtown business had once stood. The pavement went right up against a three-story brick wall. You could clearly see the outline of the missing original structure traced on the wall in front of us. White paint couldn't hide the scars from where the old structure had been demolished nor did it completely hide the original advertising for the hardware store that had once occupied this site.

Our meeting was scheduled to start in an hour, which gave us plenty of time to get familiar with the meeting room and get set up. The 6:30 start time was chosen so the employees of the branches we were acquiring from Mega Bank ("MB") had time to close their offices and drive to this centrally located site. Our audio/video folks had arrived around 5:00 and were finishing the sound system installation when we walked into the room.

The meeting was being held in an old restaurant/bar located along Main Street. The front of the room was mostly glass and afforded a view of Main Street with the Ohio River flowing by not two hundred yards in the distance. This part of town was prone to flooding just about every spring. Coming from RB, and being located about fifty miles upriver, we understood the beauty of being along the river and the pain associated with living through the spring floods. In the back of the old restaurant was a wooden bar with several high-backed bar stools. The lighting in the room was not great, but it was adequate. We set up the seating for our meeting with the guests' chairs facing the back of the room. A table was placed by the entry where we could register each person as they arrived and provided them with an information packet prepared by RB's human resources department. As I pointed out earlier, the selection of this location was specifically designed for its direct contrast to the MB culture. Their meeting facilities were big, new, high-tech, and all about MB. Keep in mind that everything you do, everything, can be used to help change a culture. We already know that momentum, capacity for change, is created when actual results align with established intent. Momentum is also created when actual results align with pre-existing expectations. That was the case here. By choosing this particular location for the meeting, we created an environment that reinforced the contrast between MB and RB, feeding their expectations for a different, hopefully better future for their Core (customers, community, and culture). Choosing this location and this setting sent the message that RB was focused on the MB team, their communities, and their customers. RB understood them and their Core.

> *Momentum is created when actual results align with established intent and when results align with pre-existing expectations.*

In keeping with the contrasting environment created for this first meeting, if I had taken the standard executive approach to my conversation with the MB group, I would have been sending confusing signals to the audience, which would have served to reduce momentum. Once I chose this location for the sake of contrast, I was committed to a contrasting presentation. I needed to deliver a non-standard, high-touch, and transparent presentation, which was consistent with the strategic approach to RB's customer-focused, balanced-growth process. I had proposed this strategic initiative weeks earlier, and it was supported by the executive committee of the board and Mr. E.

As the MB employees began to arrive, Anna and Jill, the two RB team members traveling with me, greeted and registered each guest. I had assumed my usual spot across the room and away from the activity, so I could watch the body language of the MB employees as they entered the room. Whether facial expressions or body language, I was looking for any clue regarding their current mindset. Nothing jumped out at me. The group was clearly tense and apprehensive. You would be too if you had just learned that your workplace was going to be sold to another bank. Who are these people? What happens next? Will I still have a job? All great questions, and all questions I was ready to address.

You already know that the key point here was what I did not observe. I did not see the signs of anger that would be a normal reaction if they had been told of the pending reduction in force. If I had been busy reviewing my notes or spending my time greeting people as they walked in the door, I would have had no chance to observe that critical piece of missing information. This is just another benefit from growing the people around you. Anna's and Jill's growth provided me with additional capacity. They gave me the opportunity to spend the time observing the MB employees as they entered the meeting. Use these opportunities wisely.

Promptly at 6:30, I walked to the front of the group and began what was certain to be an interesting evening.

"Good evening everyone. I am Rob. The first thing I want to do is thank you for being here this evening. Thank you for your time and your attention. Both are valuable and I promise not to waste either.

I am the controller for RB, but most importantly, you need to know that I am the guy responsible for this meeting. If you want to know who to blame for your world being turned upside down because of this acquisition, you don't have to look any further; it's me (and I held up my right hand above my head). *Don't get angry with your branch managers or your regional manager. All of these discussions took place over the last few months between myself and various executives within MB. We are here tonight to answer all your questions as best we can.*

I made it personal from the very beginning. I am Rob, not Mr. Walters, not Rob Walters, controller for RB, just Rob. Again, it was an opportunity to contrast the RB culture with the MB culture. But, there was much more to it than just the contrast of cultures. I was announcing intent so that if/when I had the chance, later in the meeting, to take the blame for a negative result, I would begin creating momentum.

"Here with me this evening are Anna and Jill. Anna is part of our human resources team and is here to go over the information packet you received when you walked in. Jill leads our conversion team. She is the person who will be taking care of the conversion process, from converting your customers' deposit balances to making certain everyone gets replacement checks. Between the three of us, we should be able to address most of your questions this evening." I immediately placed Anna and Jill on a par with me. The message was that we were all in this together. But, when it came time to take risk, that was mine and mine alone.

> *When it came time to take risk, that was mine and mine alone.*

"If we know the answers, we will tell you. We are here to provide you with full transparency regarding any topic that concerns you: your family, your customers, or your branch. If we don't know the answers to your questions, we'll tell you 'we don't know,' and we will get back to you with the answer. The phone number, directly into my office, is (xxx) xxx-xxxx, and

my company cell number is (xxx) xxx-xxxx. I am available anytime to every-one: employees, customers, and shareholders. You will find my numbers, as well as Anna's and Jill's direct numbers, listed on the second page of the packet you received when you walked in.

"Just as we will answer all of your questions to the best of our ability, we will also tell you if the subject you are asking about is none of your business. We are both (MB and RB) *SEC registered, publicly traded companies. Some of the details related to this transaction are not public information and need to remain confidential. It is just that simple. We will tell you whatever we know, and when we can't give you the answer, we will tell you that too.*

"I know this level of transparency is not what you are accustomed to, but for RB, it is part of who we are. We are not just providing financial services to these markets; we are part of our communities. This area is our home. RB's culture has evolved over the last one hundred years to reflect the culture of the people we serve. That is one of the reasons why we have been so successful. We have constructed a business model that has respect at its core. We respect the needs of our customers, our shareholders, and our team members. These are the elements that form the core of RB's culture." I was announcing intent, setting the expectation for transparency at every step, while at the same time, we were establishing acceptable boundaries. I was announcing intent that would pair with an aligned result during the meeting, building additional momentum for future transformation.

"I like things simple, and as you have already figured out, I like to be straight-forward. If you want to know something, just ask me. One of the questions I get most often during these types of meetings is: 'What is it like to work at RB?' That is a great question and here is the best way I have found to answer that question: 'There are three rules you must remember at all times, only three. Rule #1 is to be professional, which begins with respect for the customer, your team members, and yourself. Rule #2 is to work smarter, not harder. How many hours you work doesn't impress me at all. What you have accomplished during those hours is what matters. And Rule #3, maintain balance in life, have fun!" More contrast. This time, I was contrasting RB's focus on people, the people in RB's Core, with MB's focus on financial performance.

"That's it. Pretty simple. I know you have a bunch of questions this evening, so let's start with Anna, and she will cover the HR packets in front of you. After Anna covers the HR material, Jill will give you a brief description of how the conversion process works and what your customers will need to know. After they go over their materials for this evening, we will open the discussion up to your questions. You can ask anything that is on your mind, and we will do our best to give you the answer.

"Anna, the floor is yours. Oh, by the way folks, Anna and Jill are good people. They know their pieces in this process very well. I respect them and I trust their judgment, and you can too. Anna…" <u>When you have good people, get out of their way and let them do their jobs. Give them the opportunity to succeed or fail. Provide them with the opportunity to learn and grow.</u>

> *When you have good people, get out of their way and let them do their jobs.*

With that being said, I handed the mic to Anna and sat down on one of the bar stools. She spent about thirty minutes going over the prepared HR materials. Jill's presentation followed. It was shorter and very broad in scope. She took about fifteen minutes to give the group an outline of how the process would work and an approximate timeline for the conversion.

Anna was the consummate HR professional. She had a natural ability to project both understanding and empathy. Her tone and demeanor were always reassuring, and she had the anticipated calming effect on the group. Anna was the go-to person in HR. If you wanted to get something done, see Anna. She never wanted the spotlight, which worked well because her boss was one who was always in search of center stage. This was our second or third M&A presentation together and, by far, our largest group to date. As we worked through the various M&A presentations, Anna's skills had grown rapidly, and on this particular evening, she knocked it out of the park. By far, this was her best presentation.

She immediately connected with the audience and kept their attention for the entire thirty minutes.

When Jill took the floor, the group was fully engaged. They had entered the room this evening with a clear and understandable chip on their shoulders. So far, we had been true to our word. Out of respect, we had not wasted their time nor was their attention going unrewarded. Jill did her usual great job.

She had wrapped up her overview, and it was now time to open the floor to questions from the group. I stood up and turned off the mic. Previous experience had taught me that speaking without a microphone, in small groups like this one, serves to make the conversation more personal; also, it forces the audience to focus more intently on what is being said. It is much like when people naturally strain to hear a whisper but ignore someone who is shouting. My voice carries well, and I had developed the habit of repeating the questions being asked. The key is to make certain everyone can hear the questions being asked and the answers being given. I had taken my suit jacket off and loosened my tie, signaling to the group that it was time to get down to business. It was just the MB group and me. All of these non-verbals were deliberate, but they were also a true reflection of who I am. People are smart, smarter than you give them credit for. They can always recognize the difference between an act put on for effect and sincerity. This is who I was then and who I am now. Every day, I make the *choice* to be that person.

People are smart, smarter than you give them credit for. They can always recognize the difference between an act put on for effect and sincerity.

"*Let's get started. What is on your mind?*" was my invitation to the group to start the Q&A session. I was waiting for one question in particular. It was the reason I was here for this meeting. Up to this point, other than providing a name and a face for them to blame for their world being upended, Anna and Jill had delivered all of the useful information. I didn't have to wait long. After an awkward minute or two of silence within the group, here it came. They asked the question I had been waiting to hear: *"Am I going to lose my job?"*

Everything that had been done up to this point, including the environment, the expectations, the hours of preparation, all of it was designed to generate enough momentum for some form of that question to be asked. Much of the future success of this transaction rested on my ability to effectively deal with this issue. Most leaders have been taught to minimize their exposure to these types of questions or to avoid them altogether. A leader focused on establishing momentum for cultural transformation lives for moments like this. Sometimes you handle it correctly and sometimes not. In either case, you own the result. Learn from the experience, then share what you have learned with others. You can't have the opportunity to learn if you are not leading from the front. You must be willing to accept the consequences from the results.

Being that particular question was the first one out of the box told me that we had been successful in establishing the beginnings of a relationship with this group. We had been able to establish a sense of trust, project integrity, and successfully communicate our message (the three elements necessary for establishing any form of relationship). Now came the moment for me to contrast myself and, by extension, to contrast the RB culture with the MB culture. My answer was clear and to the point, which shocked the assembled group and clearly took Anna by surprise. I queried back: *"Is your job in the proof department?"* Never assume. Always be gathering more facts and additional information. The individual answered back in a loud, clear voice with a challenging tone: *"Yes, I work in the proof department and so do a bunch of us here tonight. Will we still have our jobs?"* It was the tone used when asking this question that was critical, not the question itself. What I was about to find out was MB's employees had been told one thing by MB's management, but they actually expected the truth to be different. I still had much to learn, and I would be granted access to the next piece of the puzzle if I struck the right tone with my response.

"No." I answered in a definitive but empathetic tone. "If you are employed in the proof department, about four months after the acquisition is complete, all proof functions will be consolidated into one of our existing proof departments." (FYI: One of the existing proof operation centers was about thirty minutes away from where we were meeting, and the other was about an hour away.) Either center could absorb the MB workflow, and these folks knew that. That is why there was a tone of challenge in her voice. People are always more aware than what you give them credit for.

I answered a direct question with a direct answer, which was followed by enough details for them to have a time horizon and a reasonable explanation for why the jobs would be lost. I could have danced around her question and given her standard corporate double-talk like: "Thank you for asking that question. As you know, a transaction of this type is complicated, and there are many variables to be considered. For me to provide an answer to your question this evening, at this early stage in the process, would be premature. As we get further down the road, closer to the date of conversion, we will make a final determination regarding the proof department. Let me assure you that RB values each of our team members... bla, bla, bla." If I had given the standard corporate response, I would have lost every bit of created momentum. But, by respecting a direct question with an open, honest, and empathetic direct response, I earned the right to continue on collecting more information.

There was an audible grumbling which rose up from the group and an immediate exchange of inaudible comments between the folks in the audience. After about thirty seconds had passed, a young man seated toward the back of the room stood up and in a clear voice began to address me: "Mr. Walters, Rob, I am Tim, the manager of the ABC branch and the people employed in the proof department are my employees. We have been told that no one was going to lose their job as a result of MB selling these branches to RB. Now you are telling us that we are going to lose our jobs! What are we supposed to believe?"

"Did everyone hear Tim's comments and question?" I asked the group. The group responded with a collective "yes," so I continued. *"Thank you, Tim, for your honesty and for respecting those you work with enough to stand up on their behalf. I know that wasn't easy for you to do."* <u>My comment was sincere and all about showing respect.</u> I paused long enough to drag my stool, separating it from Anna and Jill, and placed it in the center/front of the group. The act of separating my stool from Anna and Jill was intentional and designed to focus the discussion that was about to take place on one, and only one person, me. <u>Remember what I said earlier, this part was all on me not on them. Physically separating myself from Anna and Jill signaled that I, and only I, owned the consequences.</u>

Again, holding up my right hand above my head I began: *"As I said earlier, I am the guy responsible for turning your world upside down.* <u>Again, delivering results aligned with intent. Another opportunity for us to build momentum.</u> *When I say that I am responsible, I mean that I am the guy who negotiated with MB's executive team establishing the terms and conditions of this transaction. I actually wrote much of the language in the legal documents that govern this transaction, and I am responsible to RB's board and shareholders for the actual results from our future together. No one person knows the details of this deal better than I, and no one has more tied to its future success, or failure, than I. So, believe me when I tell you that there was never a representation from RB that the proof department would remain in operation, post-closing. In fact, during the negotiations, I made it very clear that it is and was always our intention to merge your proofing functions with the existing RB proof departments."* At this point, you could have heard a pin drop in the room. As you can imagine, the entire group was fully engaged. <u>The words delivered transparency, as promised. Also, the silence, due to their engagement, signaled their willingness to listen, really listen to what I had to say. Our presentation was getting through their filters and being perceived as containing substance. If they had been fidgeting or talking among themselves, it would have been a clear signal that I had more work to do in order to form a solid connection with the group.</u>

At that moment, a random comment was aired by someone in the group: *"So they lied to us again."* <u>This statement was a gift, an opportunity</u>

for me to show the MB culture some respect. If I choose to attack the MB culture through the use of disrespect, I would create emotion but not momentum. I immediately responded with: *"I doubt it. It's possible, but I imagine it is more likely a miscommunication that occurred somewhere between the MB executives that negotiated this deal and the MB manager that delivered the message. This type of thing happens all the time. I apologize for the confusion, but that is why we are talking this evening. We are here to answer your questions and address any concerns you may have. My main objective for this evening was to get to this discussion regarding the future of the proof department. May I take just a few minutes to share with you how and why these decisions were made?"* Asking permission is an excellent tool for leaders to use when building momentum. When you feel the connection has been made with the audience, continue to show them respect through seeking their permission on an issue. Ask permission to continue speaking for a little while longer, change topics in order to raise what may be an uncomfortable topic, or do something as simple as taking off your suit jacket. They are small things, but all of these small things add up to big opportunities.

I continued: *"You and I are all in this together. If this goes badly, it is my fault and my fault alone. If our efforts are successful, you are the*

> *Results and intent had aligned multiple times in just a few minutes and momentum overtook apprehension and focus shifted to the future.*

folks that made it happen, and you will get all of the credit. Let me share just a brief snapshot of our vision of what we can accomplish for our customers and the communities we serve...." When these words were spoken, they were accepted as fact. One could sense that the MB audience was beginning to hold this pending transaction up to the light and see the different colors. This is when the audience shifted from "What's going on?" to "What's going to happen next?" Results and intent had aligned multiple times in just a few minutes and momentum overtook apprehension. Their focus shifted to the future. Cultural transformation had begun.

With those words being spoken, a calm settled over the group, and for the first time in a long time, they felt like they were going to become part of a team. They had an opportunity to help shape their own futures. They had been given something they had not expected, that being the honesty that comes from respect, combined with a clear sense of purpose.

I went on to explain to the group that no one involved in direct customer contact would be displaced. I also explained that within the business model which we used to project the financial results from their region over the next eighteen months, we had built in the cost of hiring additional branch employees. This brought a collective comment from the group: *"Thank heavens. We are way understaffed in the branches."* I also shared with them RB's use of technology. We had spent the last few years building what was, for that point in time, a new type of data management system. RB's systems were designed to put the power of technology in the hands of the end user and take it out of the hands of the backroom, mainframe programmers. I challenged them to learn these new concepts quickly because we had found that with this new power in the hands of the frontline employees, customers were very pleased with the improved flexibility and speed of service. Our leveraging technology to better serve our customers had been the reason why RB was able to quickly grow market share. We had grown, not because of price, but due to the quality of service (value) being delivered to the customer.

When you have earned momentum, don't waste it. Be prepared to put it to work immediately. When I teach leaders about strategic planning, I always remind them to have a plan for success. Every executive I have ever worked with had at least a "Plan B" for when something went wrong. Some even have a C and D ready to go, just in case. Do you realize how few executives have a plan ready for leveraging the momentum created by success? Answer: Not many. My purpose within this section was not to tell the MB group how RB had grown. My purpose was to let them know how they were going to grow. I had their attention. I needed to leverage the momentum and let them know what was in it for them, their families, their communities, and their customers.

As we were wrapping up the meeting, I added: *"I want to make this one final point. We have a challenging four or five months ahead of us. There will be problems, and you will become frustrated. Call me whenever you need to, but more importantly, talk with each other. Help each other. For those of you who choose to leave, I certainly understand and will support you any way I can. If you choose to stay with us over the next six months, there will be a retention bonus. Anna will be able to give you the details. For those of you in the proof department, you will be given strong consideration for any positions that open up in the branches and in the existing proof departments. If you are employed as a proof operator and stay with us during this transaction, you will receive a severance package as part of your termination, which will be based on your accumulated years of service. Is that fair?"* The answer came back in the form of smiles from the group and an audible, collective murmur of *"yes"* and *"thank you."*

> *Very few executives have a plan ready for leveraging the momentum created by success.*

"Thank you for your time and attention this evening. I am looking forward to working with each of you. We will stay around for a little while if you have any questions. Please be safe going home. Good night." And with that, the presentation ended. These last two sections were all about transparency and respect, and letting them know that RB had already been planning for their futures. The warning about future difficulty was nothing more than stating the obvious, but the way it was framed created a future team building opportunity. When the inevitable problems arise, the negative results will align with the announced intent, creating momentum. The additional momentum will help them to get through the challenges ahead. By the time they face the conversion-related issues, they will have already been taught to see problems as opportunities to learn. There is

no downside for the MB team, which is by design. After all, I have taken responsibility for anything that goes wrong. We have created a win-win-win for all three members of the RB Core. In total, we spent around ninety minutes in front of the MB group. The lines for questions formed immediately but very few questions were directed toward me. The MB folks wanted to talk to Anna and Jill. This reaction was the best I could have hoped for. This mix of follow-up questions was a clear indication that their focus was on the future. They wanted to know what came next and, most importantly, how they could help. A wonderful result!

What else came out of that meeting? Well, there were several additional points of interest from that evening. When we got in the car to drive home, no one said anything for a little while, then I asked: *"Well, how do you think that went?"* Jill spoke first and commented on all she had learned about their existing systems. She was shocked by how far behind MB was in the application of new technology. Jill saw this as a great opportunity to help the new employees to better serve their customers. Jill was spot-on. That nugget of information proved to be a major factor in RB rapidly gaining post-transaction market share. The successful results from these locations created additional momentum for us to incorporate new, customer-focused technologies within our existing branches. When viewed by others, success breeds success (momentum creates capacity).

Here is where we stop our review of the MB meeting and expanding on the opportunities to learn, opportunities that are found everywhere, once you know how to perceive them. The conversation during the rest of the trip home that evening was centered on RB's cultural politics. It is the normal stuff we all deal with every day. Here are the two primary takeaways from the remaining dialog between Anna and me. One, I had a well-established strategic plan for success in place with the support of RB's most senior leadership. And, two, I knew from the insights found within Anna's questions that she had grown as a leader and was now seeing more of the colors when opportunity is held up to the light. She would go on to help Jill grow and would be a positive influence on all RB team members with whom she came into contact. It was a great evening!

Cultural Transformation:
One Nation, Two Cultures, Three Generations.

We have learned how cultures are constructed and influenced at the Kitchen Table, the Boardroom, and within our Communities, but what about culture on a national level? How are national cultures constructed, influenced, and transformed? The answer is doing it the same way. The same concepts and models apply to all cultural groups, including the United States of America (Our Nation). There are differences due to the geographic size and the scope of interconnected complexities (global versus family), but the concepts and driving forces underlying cultural development and change are the same, regardless of size. The good news is once you have developed the skills for leading cultural change, those same skills apply at every level.

The concepts and driving forces underlying cultural development and change are the same, regardless of size.

Allow me to frame this discussion with the following. Consider this statement: "In my personal opinion, the current state of our national politics and political system is silly and very dangerous." I can easily make an argument that the vast majority of Our Nation's population would agree with my statement. How can I assume that most would agree with me? As you have learned, ideology can be based on actual results (Results to the power of Intent), or ideology can be based on intent alone (the acceptable perception of facts). So, it is safe for me to assume that a significant percentage of Our Nation's population would perceive my statement as true when viewed from the results side, plus there will be a significant percentage that would view my statement as true viewing it from the intent side? Now that we have established "The other side is the one that is silly and dangerous," how can we begin to bridge the communication gap that has been intentionally constructed between the two polarized ideologies?

Step one is to better understand the three basic methods of cultural change: manipulation, transition, and transformation. Each method can take different forms during the change process, but there are basic characteristics by which each method can be identified.

Let's define each in terms of ideology used, capacity created, and primary influences applied by the cultural leaders.

1. Manipulation—Cultural change by manipulation is the primary method applied by the intent-based ideology. An intent-based ideology creates no momentum for change during its application. The capacity for change must be created within the population through leadership's triggering emotional responses and imposing various forms of restriction. In order for a single leader or a small group of leaders to effect manipulation, they must maintain an ever-increasing level of Command and Control over the population.

2. Transition—Cultural change by transition is the most common method applied by the results-based ideology when the ideology is defined by the formula: Results to the power of Intent. Transitional change performed under this formula creates momentum within the population based on the alignment of actual results with stated intent, creating the perception of enhanced future value. Momentum creates capacity for change within the population, which is enhanced by leadership's use of transparency and rewarding individual accomplishment.

3. Transformation—Transformation is less frequently applied, but it is the most dynamic method of cultural change. It is applied by the results-based ideology when the ideology is defined by the formula: Results to the power of Understanding. Transformational change performed under this formula creates momentum within the population based on the alignment of actual results with the population's understanding of the stated goal, creating

the existence of self-determination and unlimited future value. Momentum creates a renewing capacity for change within the population, which is enhanced by leadership's use of respect and understanding, placing the needs of the culture ahead of their own needs. In addition to the cornerstones of respect and understanding, transformation requires transparency, the guaranteed freedom of choice, and the rewarding of individual innovation.

The Learning Model is located at the base of all leadership and understanding forms its foundation. The Transformational Leadership Model, Illustration #11.f, was constructed with Results at the top, using the qualifiers of Quality and Financial. Understanding creates the foundation for all Results. That is the Transformational Leadership Model for the results-based ideology. My approach to leadership has always been results-based, but to be successful at cultural transformation, I needed to understand and be able to work effectively within the intent-based model as well.

To change the Transformational Leadership Model so that it illustrates the intent-based ideology, we reduce the required support from understanding

> *My approach to leadership has always been results-based, but to be successful at cultural transformation, I needed to understand the intent-based model as well.*

and replace the ultimate goal of leadership from Results to Intent. With Intent at the top, still using the qualifiers of Quality and Financial, we have now constructed the Intent-based Leadership Model. See Illustration #12 below.

Please note that it is Intent which is now balanced on the point of perception formed by customers and shareholders and supported by the Culture. Also notice that the Intent qualifier, Finance, is weighted more

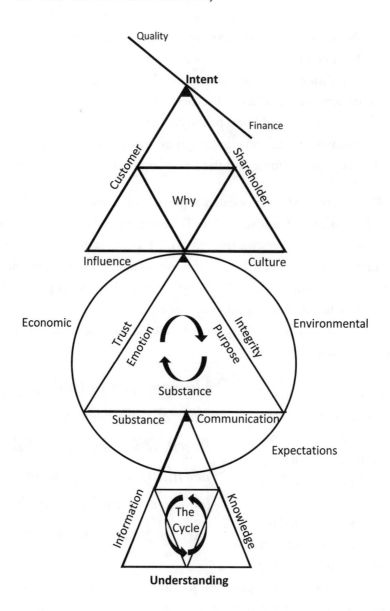

heavily than Quality, indicating that the focus of the Stakeholders (the Leaders) rests on themselves, with little to no regard for the Quality of the impact on the customer. This is always the case when the Intent-based Leadership Model is applied.

How does changing a single word in the model change cultural leadership? Both versions of the model illustrate cultural change, right? Yes, both are effective ways of changing culture. The difference is in how the change is designed to take place. Think back to our two different formulas for truth. <u>Truth is</u> = acceptable perceived facts. <u>The Truth</u> = the sum of ({Experienced Facts} + {Proven Facts} + {Believed Facts}). If Intent sits at the top of the model, development still takes place by providing transparency. Only this time, the Universe of Present Facts has been restricted to include only those facts perceived to be acceptable to the ideology.

At the heart of the Learning Model, the model that forms the base for both results-based and intent-based leadership, the Cycle is working to feed the support structure by providing substantive communication. But, under the Intent-based Leadership Model, the Cycle will be running learning loops against a set of restricted facts. Each time the loop returns for more data, it will have access to only those facts deemed to be acceptable. So, all transparency within the intent-based model, from the foundation up, is restricted to data supporting the acceptable

> *The intent-based model marginalizes or even demonizes any result which is contrary to the established, declared intent.*

Intent. The sharing of unauthorized knowledge is discouraged, as is the sharing of nonconforming experiences. The intent-based model marginalizes or even demonizes any result which is contrary to the established, declared intent. The culture developed under an intent-based ideology ultimately views The Truth as equal to the sum of <u>acceptable</u> ({Experienced Facts} + {Proven Facts} + {Believed Facts}). Notice in Illustration #12 how restricted the foundation of understanding has become. The entire leadership model has become top-heavy and much less stable than the Transformational Leadership Model.

Intent-based manipulation produces no momentum for change because there is no alignment of declared intent with actual results; therefore, there is no creation of perceived future value within the population.

In fact, intent-based manipulation actually serves to reduce the capacity for change within the culture. However, change must be accomplished in order for the culture to survive, so in the place of momentum, capacity for change is created by continuously improving efficiency. Continuously improving efficiencies are produced through a combination of increased regulation and additional restrictions. Putting it another way, there will be more and more laws, regulations, policies, and procedures imposed in the name of efficiency. Under the intent-based model, uncontrolled innovation and all other individual freedoms are viewed as inefficiencies because they are nonconforming aberrations within the population. These unsanctioned, individual activities must be restricted because they are viewed as less efficient than a centralized (national) Command and Control structure.

As a result of the increased restrictions placed on the Cycle of Human Development by an intent-based ideology, subsequent generations will have less and less access to unauthorized knowledge. At first, a small percentage of the population will perceive increased restriction as a welcomed structure, creating order within an otherwise chaotic world. These accepting members will concentrate their efforts toward compliance with the established intent. The other, much larger percentage of the population will reject or ignore the increased restrictions. Instead, this independent group will continue to cling to their results-based ideology supporting innovation and individual freedoms.

We now have the formation of a communication gap between the two divergent ideologies. The more restrictive the intent-based ideology becomes, the more resolute the results-based ideology. Over time, the differing approaches to transformational leadership create the silly and dangerous environment we discussed earlier, producing the Haves and the Have-nots.

Counter to accepted theory, I offer the following for your consideration. The existing communication gap between the Haves and the Have-nots is not based on political party affiliation, Democrat versus Republican, nor is it a function of conservative versus progressive. Our

Nation's two-culture environment is not a function of differing ethnic backgrounds or economic statuses nor is it driven by the color of one's eyes. These divisive identifiers are only a few examples. There are dozens of emotional subdivisions which have been created as a way to justify the need for ever-increasing restrictions. More examples of divisive identifiers include: gender preferences, immigration status, climate change, abortion, religious preference, and the list grows daily. None of these subdivisions form the cause of our two-culture Nation. The growing division between the Haves and the Have-nots is a communication gap existing between those within Our Nation holding a results-based ideology and those holding an intent-based ideology.

Commonly referred to today as "Identity Politics," the use of these emotional subdivisions serve absolutely no practical purpose other than to trigger pre-programmed, emotional responses within the ideologies. Why use them?

> *The growing division between the Haves and the Have-nots is a communication gap existing between those holding a results-based ideology and those holding an intent-based ideology.*

Remember, emotion is one of the catalysts within any productive relationship and is tied to the element of Trust. If I can trigger a negative emotional reaction within you, your level of distrust will be immediately elevated. If I can create a level of distrust followed by a steady stream of substantive communication supporting the distrust I just created, I can effectively control the future success or failure of the relationship. It is especially easy to manipulate a collective relationship (a culture) when it has been educated to hold a heightened sensitivity toward emotional subdivision terminology. Also, adding to the ease and speed of cultural manipulation is a reduction in the number of direct/personal experiences shared, while increasing the number of indirect/virtual experiences within the population.

These emotional subdivisions will result in an increased communication gap based at its core on a lack of shared, common human experiences. Shared human experiences create reference points for the perception of purpose (integrity) which are built into the relationship to allow enough time for communication to re-establish trust. We know from Book 1 that the absence of shared human experiences creates an inability to anticipate the actions of another, fostering a lack of trust between the cultures and triggering an enhanced application of the relationship catalyst emotion. Deliberately injecting emotional subdivisions into an environment where trust is already lacking or integrity (purpose) has already been called into question accelerates the deterioration of the relationship. The lack of shared human experiences creates a gap in substantive communication, slowing or stopping the healing process. The use of emotional subdivisions is the essence of cultural manipulation.

> *The use of emotional subdivisions is the essence of cultural manipulation.*

This form of cultural change is effective, easily accomplished, and as old as humanity itself.

How would an outside observer know if there was a communication gap forming between the Haves and Have-nots? First, one would see a growing intolerance for independent thought or nonconforming action. In the beginning, this intolerance will be directed inward at the individual members of the culture in order to create uniformity and acceptance of dominant ideology. Eventually, after uniformity is achieved, intolerance will be directed outward toward the opposing ideology. The root cause for intolerance will be constructed around a perceived threat to the basic human *need* for security within either culture for the Haves, as well as the Have-nots. Those holding a results-based ideology will see those with an intent-based ideology as a threat to their future security and vice versa. These perceptions, based in the truth or not, will be intensified over time as the leaders leverage the catalyst of emotion to further divide the two cultures.

Divide and conquer. Create distrust in an enemy, demonize them, and then rally behind (create momentum for) defeating the enemy. This approach to cultural manipulation is extremely effective. In order to succeed, it only requires a complacent or dependent population which has been consistently misinformed or is willingly uneducated.

In all of human history, the struggle for control over cultural ideology, results-based versus intent-based, has always begun with one side gaining influence over the Cycle. The earlier in the human development process you can begin reinforcing the chosen ideology, the more efficient and effective the propaganda. Recall the Learning Model. In order to create substantive communication, one must successfully maneuver through the Filtration, Selection, and Listening processes. Historically, the most efficient way for leaders to leverage the elements of communication is to gain control over the content being taught during the formative years of youth, prior to high school graduation.

Under intent-based cultural manipulation, additional changes with more restrictive changes will be put into place over the subsequent generations. Within two or three birth generations, the Universe of Present Facts being taught to the new group of young people is almost unrecognizable when compared

> *The communication gap grows with each subsequent generation, serving to further polarize the competing ideologies.*

to the Present Facts that were taught to their grandparents. The communication gap grows, expanding exponentially, with each subsequent generation, serving to further polarize the competing ideologies. Do you know when the United States Department of Education (USDE) was formed, formalizing the centralized control of the Our Nation's education process? Late 1800s? No. Surprisingly, the USDE was formed in October 1979 by President Carter. Just for additional perspective, here are some other extremely powerful federal agencies which hold tremendous regulatory control over our daily lives: Environmental Protection Agency, December 1970, President Nixon; Occupational Safety and Health Administration, April 1971, President Nixon; and the Department of Homeland Security, November 2002, President George W. Bush. Given this book is being written in 2019 and using the average of 25.5 years as the birth generation gap, these four examples of massive regulatory agencies have been put into place within the last 1.9 generations.

What my mother and father were taught in school during the 1930s differed significantly **in content** from what I was taught during the late 1960s and early 1970s, simply due to the pace of human advancement from one generation to the next. What our son was taught during the late 1990s and early 2000s, the third generation, differed **both in content and the acceptable perception of fact,** due to the rapid advancement of intent-based ideology.

The social aspects of the public educational process for my son's generation had evolved from the normal peer pressures I experienced to peer pressure plus political correctness. As his generation was growing up, they faced new cultural influences (environmental, economic, and expectations) from peers regarding acceptable actions and choices. But, his generation was the first to also face significant, additional restrictions on acceptable thought and opinion. These restrictions were labeled "political correctness" and are being imposed within the secondary educational system (grades K-twelve). The Truth was well on its way to becoming the acceptable perception of fact as defined by cultural leaders and enforced through the use of emotional subdivisions.

How can a handful of cultural leaders, known and unknown (meaning elected officials and bureaucrats), be so efficient in controlling the perceptions of a population? Again, this is nothing new. In the history of humanity, there has always been a centralized group of leaders more than willing to seize power over differing populations and exercise centralized influence. Within the United States of America, the influence over our culture is granted by the voter to the government. Our leaders and those that support them have specific functions as defined by our Constitution and Bill of Rights. The design of Our Nation's founding documents limits the power of government, protecting an individual's freedom of choice and their pursuit of purpose. So, how can Our Nation's cultural leaders gain a controlling influence when the documents are in place to protect the population against this very action? You now know the answer to that question. The way this manipulation has been accomplished is through the tried-and-true use of social intimidation (emotion and fear), propaganda, and the indoctrination of the population's youth.

What is new is the speed at which the manipulation has taken place. The change of Our Nation's culture over the last forty years, when compared to the pace of change within previous generations, is directly attributed to the intelligent leveraging of rapidly evolving technology, including the use of automated search engines and informational tools. When you look at the practical application of today's informational loops and data searches, they can all take place in seconds, making it possible to access a vast expanse of Present Facts at any time and from virtually any location. Certainly, this is an unlimited opportunity for learning. But, there are only a handful of automated search engines available for use when accessing the available Present Facts. The interworkings (programmed algorithms) used by these search engines are written and maintained by only a select few. The vast majority of us using these wonderful tools have no idea how they work.

Heard any news recently about bias within the companies that develop and maintain these automated engines and tools? These boardroom cultures are heavily weighted toward the intent-based ideology. Think of it this way: If I control the Present Facts you have access to and manage the methods used to search, extract, and format that information, I ultimately control a significant portion of your post-secondary school development. If my development bias is an intent-based ideology and the educational system you are exposed to as you mature is also aligned with my bias, your ideological development will almost certainly be intent-based. When you exit the controlled, intent-based environment and enter the reality of a results-based environment, your intent-based ideology may begin to slowly evolve as shared experiences begin to replace previous indoctrination.

The use of social intimidation, propaganda, and the indoctrination of the young are as old school as it gets. These tools have been around forever, just in the manual form. Recall my cautioning you earlier about when you search through a massive pile of garbage, no matter how quickly your search engine affects the selection process, you are going to end up selecting garbage. These intent-based influences are all working together, resulting in a speed and a depth of manipulation which is way beyond the scope of any prior cultural change process.

> *At all cultural levels, intent-based ideology fails to produce long-term tangible results.*

At the end of the day, all of these factors have combined to outstrip the ability of our centralized leaders (elected officials and bureaucrats) to keep up with the pace of change. How do I know this is the truth? Look at the actual results. At all cultural levels, intent-based ideology fails to produce long-term tangible results. As time goes on, a culture built on a progressively more intent-based ideology grows. There is never enough revenue generated to fund the list of wants offered by the leaders or demanded by the population. The consistent need of the culture to borrow funds from the future to pay for the present is one of the unmistakable signs of a solidly entrenched intent-based ideology, and this is true at the Kitchen Table, Boardroom, and Community levels. Let's test my conclusion by using Our Nation as an example.

To date, Our Nation has borrowed an accumulated total of $22 trillion ($22,000,000,000,000). That means Our Nation's leaders have spent or have committed to spend $22 trillion more than they have collected from us in the form of taxes. And, at the current pace of annual debt, that number will grow by almost $1 trillion each year for the next ten years. So, let's examine the actual results from the spending of all that borrowed money which, by the way, represents the total of money borrowed and spent by our federal government in addition to the $3 to $4 trillion of tax revenues collected annually.

We don't need to go back more than the last two birth generations to make the point. In 1965, after Congress passed a set of domestic programs known as the Great Society, President Lyndon Johnson signed them into law. The Great Society was a set of programs with the stated intent of totally eliminating poverty and racial injustice in Our Nation. In 1971, President Nixon declared War on Drugs with the intent of stopping the flow of illegal drugs into Our Nation, especially the flow coming in over our southern border. President Obama signed and Congress passed almost $1 trillion of new spending, specifically intended to fix Our Nation's crumbling infrastructure. Every president from the 1980s forward has insisted on securing our southern border and slowing the pace of illegal immigration into Our Nation. President Obama signed, after Congress passed, a sweeping law to improve our health care system. Billions, if not trillions, of dollars have been spent and countless regulations imposed with the intent to improve our public education system, increase the quality of health care for veterans, secure our banking system, fund Social Security, keep Medicare solvent, etc., etc. How are all these good intentions working out for the population of Our Nation?

Please consider the following set of "result" statements. Our Nation's poverty has been almost eliminated. Racial injustices no longer exist. Our southern border has long since been secured. The War on Drugs has been won. The quality of our public education system ranks at the top of every list when compared to other developed countries. Our Nation's interstates, bridges, airports, and air traffic control systems have all been repaired and modernized. Our veterans are receiving the quality of care they deserve, and our health care system costs have gone down significantly, while our access to care has improved.

After borrowing $22 trillion, $16.6 trillion of which was borrowed over the last birth generation, and putting the massive resources of an ever-expanding federal government behind these very specific goals, one would expect the results from the paragraph above to be mostly true. Clearly, none of these issues have been resolved and many would say that most of the social and infrastructure issues listed above have not improved and may have gotten worse in the last twenty-five years.

Allow me to continue making my point. Remember, all cultures work the same. Consider the impact of intent-based ideology on Community. What has happened to the quality of life in many of Our Nation's larger cities? What about in your community? How about the culture found in Our Nation's boardrooms? Consider the lessons learned (or not learned) after Enron, WorldCom, the dot-com bubble, the housing bubble, and the Great Recession. How would you assess the strength and stability of Our Nation's family unit today (the culture gathered around the Kitchen Table) compared to this same culture two generations ago?

We started this review as a response to the question of: "How do I know that the pace of change has outstripped the ability of our centralized leaders to keep up with the pace of change?" Please look around you and actually see what has happened. This is yet another opportunity to "view the duck from both perspectives." All of these results and hundreds more serve to support the conclusion that leadership under an intent-based ideology cannot be sustained without creating massive restriction and massive debt. Why? Because intent-based ideology, by definition, is designed to first create, then maintain an

> *Intent-based ideology, by definition, is designed to first create, then maintain an issue.*

issue. This cycle of fabricated need keeps the population in fear of future security and reduces their ability to achieve the luxury of purpose, making them easier to control.

Intent-based leaders never solve problems or create results, because results feed the Cycle, enhancing shared experiences and giving weight to Quality. Once Quality enters into the population's set expectations, curiosity kicks in, and they will be seeking more Quality enhancing results. The more weight is assigned to Quality, the more demand is created for a results-based ideology.

Can an intent-based ideology ever produce actual results? Yes, but only as an exception. The best example I can give you is when Our Nation's Armed Forces are not heavily restricted by imposed rules of engagement, they can produce amazing results. In almost every case of an intent-based ideology producing actual results, you will find an emotional catalyst at work, prompting the short-lived focus on results. Again, under intent-based ideology, too many shared results will serve to disrupt the cultural manipulation process, so leaders will keep actual, positive results to a minimum.

How did we get here? How did intent-based ideology become so influential so quickly? I don't believe that the architects of the modern-day, intent-based ideology started out with any type of forty-year strategic plan for success. Far from it. I think it simply became the path of least resistance for Our Nation's leaders.

In the 1950s, Our Nation's results-based culture was on a roll. The threats from the Great Depression and World War II had been conquered and Our Nation had just gone through a decade of transitional leadership focused on Results, with a slight imbalance toward the Finance qualifier. In the 1960s, the next generation was born into the luxury of choosing their purpose. In general terms, the *needs* for safety and security had been accomplished by the prior generation, leaving the next generation to inherit, not earn, the luxury of purpose. For their purpose, the next generation chose to rebalance the Core Model by focusing on Results with a high priority placed on the Quality qualifier. Specifically, the new generation focused on the qualities of life. Freedom of choice and social equality were two of the central themes from this period. They were simply attempting to rebalance the Results which had been tipped more toward the Finance side by the prior generation. However, this rebalancing had a much greater impact on the culture than previous rebalancing efforts. Why? Advances in technology. This time, instead of reading or hearing the accounts of protests against accepted cultural norms, the population was able to view the images and hear the actual sounds associated with these events from the convenience of their homes.

For the first time in human history, differing perspectives (views) were being delivered free to anyone who had a television set. The stark visual contrasts being offered daily between the results of the Kitchen Table culture and the results of Our Nation's culture were shocking to the population. Good people, sitting at their kitchen tables with the best of intentions and the newly acquired luxury of purpose, cried out for the leaders to right the wrongs they were now witnessing through their new window to the world. This was much like our example of the Arctic Culture when the leaders were successful in providing a stable source of heat. Once the need of security was met, the population demanded of their leaders to help other villages fix their need for reliable heat. Then, while they were doing that, the population also demanded that those same leaders fix their health care system. Remember that example? This is the same concept. The Arctic leaders, in an attempt to meet the needs of the population, stepped on the treadmill of performance and set out to accomplish what had been demanded of them. Fact: There are only twenty-four hours in a day, and you can only run uphill for so long before you have to step off. To survive, leaders need to follow Leadership Rule #2: Always strive to work smarter, not harder.

At some point, as is the case with all leaders, the demands placed on successful leadership will outstrip the leader's ability to produce the desired results. There is a point where no matter how hard or smart you work, it is not possible for you to meet the existing level of cultural expectation. This was the dilemma faced by Our Nation's leaders during the 1960s. Faced with the choice of working harder and possibly failing to meet cultural expectations or working smarter and learning to work more efficiently by leveraging the new technology, the leaders chose to work smarter. The population was calling out for balance to be restored, and if balance meant additional restrictions, then so be it. The increased restriction of an intent-based ideology was clearly the least painful leadership path available to the leaders. But, how would a population driven by a result-based ideology (expecting individual freedom and reward for innovation) react to increased restriction? Answer: The population will need to be taught that these new restrictions are acceptable and that previous perceptions regarding actual results are no longer valid or even welcome. Since the population's new demands for Quality outstripped the leadership's ability to produce solutions, the leaders focused the population on their <u>intent</u> to fix the problem. Stated intentions became the acceptable perception of success. Out of necessity, leveraging the educational system, along with the latest in technology, became the cornerstones of the new intent-based ideology.

Only within an intent-based culture can a leader be perceived as serving the interests of the population while failing to address any of the population's major expectations and then be rewarded for their failure.

As the 1960s became the 1970s, the intent-based ideology found its voice, and those progressive enough to grasp the opportunities found themselves in the beginnings of a cultural transition. Only within an intent-based culture can a leader be perceived as serving the interests of the population for decades, while failing to address any of the population's major expectations, and then be rewarded for their failure with additional personal wealth and power.

When did I first discover the existence of these two opposing ideologies and begin to realize the implications? Actually, the first time I put the basic concepts together was during my preparation for the MB transaction. I realized that MB had undergone a shift in culture. MB's culture of results and innovation was in the process of being replaced by a culture of efficiency. The Quality of results produced for the Core was being replaced with a focus on Financial results for the shareholders and a select few Stakeholders. Once I began to see this pattern develop within MB, I was able to see similar patterns developing in other companies, including RB. When I realized the nature of the cultural shift taking place within RB, I began putting into place strategic objectives that would counter or at least slow the transition. These changes worked well for the RB Core over the next few years.

The most interesting part, for me, came when I discovered that these same ideological concepts applied in every industry. When I realized how universal they were, I began pulling the flap on the tent back for other leaders by constructing the rules and models I have shared with you through these first two books (and Book 3 when it comes out in the spring of 2020). Eventually, I grew to understand that results versus intent was a part of human nature existing at all cultural levels and was not simply limited to the boardroom.

Please understand, those advocating for a results-based ideology as well as those advocating for an intent-based ideology are not evil people. Today, as during all of human history, true evil does exist in the world, but neither of these two ideologies qualify. No, the advocates for either side of this ideological struggle spend much of their time demonizing the opposing side, but the opposing view is not evil, just different. This is a concept we need to learn to appreciate, the concept of being different.

Usually, when I introduce myself to an audience for the first time, I refer to myself as being "different" in my approach to leadership. But, my being different does not make me better, nor does it make me special; I'm just different. This statement is also true for the members of the opposing ideologies; neither side is better, nor are they special. Being different, especially in the context of leadership, typically refers to the perspective(s) one holds. The ability to simultaneously see the duck from both the shore and from under the water is a skill, an understanding, developed by leaders over time. Members of the results-based ideology, as well as the members of the intent-based ideology, have not accomplished anything that is better or special. Both sides have simply developed a narrower, singular perspective (a way of understanding) which limits their ability to effectively communicate with those holding an opposing view. Based on our understanding of the Transformational Leadership Model, we now know what will develop in the absence of understanding and a lack of substantive communication, increased restriction, and growing conflict.

Ask any employer about what they must go through in order to transition high school or college graduates into contributing members of their organizations. While you are asking about educating the younger workforce, ask them how much time and money they spend dealing with state and federal regulations. Then step back! Their response will be one of frustration, fueled by emotion. You get the idea. The actual results listed by any employer is proof that we are evolving rapidly to an intent-based culture, and the change is occurring at a pace well beyond

> *The cultural change process we are experiencing is intent-based; therefore, it does not create capacity for change, only increased restrictions.*

our capacity to effectively lead the transition. Why? Because the cultural change process we are experiencing is intent-based; therefore, it does not create capacity for change, only increased restrictions.

Sooner or later, the population's tolerance for restriction will be exceeded, and the results-based ideology will re-emerge as the driving force for change. Or, as is frequently the case, the leaders will continue to accumulate power until they are effectively in control of all aspects of cultural development. At that point, we will have converted from our current Transitional Leadership type to a Terminal Leadership environment. In either case, the re-emergence of a results-based ideology or the creation of Terminal Leadership, the process of cultural change awaiting the next generation (the fourth generation), will be painful. The real question for Our Nation, since there is going to be short-term pain in either case, is what do you want to have at the end, the freedom of choice or the ever-increasing burden of compliance? I will always choose freedom.

"Those who fail to learn from history are doomed to repeat it." I have repeated that saying many times when encouraging leaders to look around and learn from the experience of others. Those who see themselves on the cutting edge of leadership are usually shocked to find out how little of what we are learning is actually new. It is just different. To help make my point about history, I usually reference two books. First, there is a book titled *The Art of War*. It is attributed to the ancient Chinese military strategist, Sun Tzu. Written in the 5th century BC, it is composed of thirteen chapters, with each chapter devoted to an aspect of warfare, military strategies, and tactics. One of the many quotes found within this book is: "If you know the enemy and know yourself, you need not fear the result of a hundred battles. If you know yourself

> *Understanding has always formed the foundation for success.*

but not the enemy, for every victory gained you will also suffer a defeat. If you know neither the enemy nor yourself, you will succumb in every battle." There are many useful takeaways from this nugget of wisdom. At the top of my list is the never-changing importance placed on our need to understand. Understanding has always formed the foundation for success on the battlefield, just as it supports every type of successful leadership or method of cultural change.

Begin by knowing/understanding yourself. At the same time, you must invest the time to know/understand those around you and the cultural influences at work creating change. The more you understand both sides, as well as the perceptions and experiences of those who oppose you, the more prepared you will be for success. Understanding only one side gives you a fifty-fifty chance of success. Not taking the time to understand either side will always result in failure. If you refuse to invest the effort needed to understand yourself and those around you, then you have chosen to exist within an intent-based ideology. By default, you have chosen to grant others control over your future, in which case you choose to follow their imposed purpose, not your own. Under these circumstances, we all lose.

There is another historical quotation which comes from the Christian Holy Bible: "Thou shalt love thy neighbor as thyself." Just as we inserted the word "understand" for the word "know" in the Sun Tzu quotation above, insert the word "respect" for the word "love" into the quotation from the Holy Bible. Now it reads: "Thou shalt respect thy neighbor as thyself." My replacing the use of the word "love" (the verb love) with the word "respect" is not meant to equate the two. However, respect is one of the results from the application of love. As we talked about in Book 1, the verb love goes beyond respect. The choice of love requires you to put yourself at risk for the benefit of others in a relentless effort to find ways to extend yourself for others, identify and meet their legitimate needs, and seek their greatest good. The verb love actually calls for us to both respect and understand those around us, seeking their greatest good. This is a great summary statement for living better and leading differently.

I am not, in any way, equating *The Art of War* and the Holy Bible. Sun Tzu wrote about how to win in battle. The various authors of the Holy Bible wrote about how to win in life and beyond. The takeaway from the use of these two quotes is that over two thousand years ago, humans were writing about the power of understanding and respect. Understanding begins with respect, Leadership Rule #1. Self-respect and respect for all of those around you is what places your feet on the path to understanding. The more you learn how to offer respect, the more understanding you will gain and the broader your foundation for Transformational Leadership. Restricting respect to only yourself or to a small group of elites narrows the path to understanding, reducing the foundation upon which Transformational Leadership rests. The less respect held for yourself and others, the narrower the foundation of understanding, and the less stability in the leadership model. An unstable leadership model must ultimately be stabilized or societal chaos will result. You can count on the leaders stabilizing the culture through one of two methods: more restriction being placed on the population (intent-based ideology) or increased levels of understanding (results-based ideology). Once again, when we refuse to learn the many lessons offered by history and fail to prioritize respect and understanding, we all lose.

> *Over two thousand years ago, humans were writing about the power of understanding and respect.*

The contents of Book 1, as well as everything in this second book, are written to help you discover the concepts, tools, and models needed to better understand the daily challenges (the battles) we all face. These first two books focus on the power of respect, understanding, and the advantages offered by learning to perceive the world of leadership differently.

LIVE better LEAD differently (Book 1) focused on how and why respect and understanding are critical in order to influence yourself and those closest to you. let's all LIVE better & LEAD differently (Book 2) focuses on continuing your leadership growth; only this time, we explored the how and why behind influencing the cultures around us and the ideologies that drive them. change to LIVE better & LEAD differently (Book 3) will focus on learning the how and why of effective change management, explaining the implementation of real change that will stand the test of time. We will also explore the role effective change management plays in creating capacity, and in influencing the individuals and cultures around us.

Book 4, if there is a Book 4, has the working title: <u>need to LIVE better & LEAD differently</u>. The current concept for the fourth book is, take all we have learned in the leadership trilogy, and apply the concepts to see what is coming at us from around the corner. We will roll time forward and discuss what the fourth generation of leadership will look like. But, that is IF Book four is written, and that is a big IF.

It is my hope that, when completed, the LIVE better LEAD differently series will serve as a catalyst for changing the conversation and the perceptions surrounding leadership. Learning to understand at a pace fast enough to keep ahead of tomorrow's evolving ideology is the challenge all leaders will face going forward.

Over the years, I have found people to be remarkably intelligent, creative, and resilient. As a leader, if you can discover a way to make an intangible challenge appear real, people will find a way to solve the problem. This trilogy is my attempt to not only make the challenges we face appear real, but to pull back the flap on the tent and let everyone see what is happening. Once people are informed through transparency designed in a way to demonstrate the "how" and the "why" behind the solution, leaders

> *The future of effective leadership is all about respect, understanding, transparency, innovation, and freedom.*

need to step out of the way, and let people get to work designing innovative solutions. The future of leadership is not Command and Control, nor is it the restriction of an intent-based ideology. The future of effective leadership is all about respect, understanding, transparency, innovation, and freedom. Those who fail to learn from history are doomed to repeat it. Never stop learning!

Thank you for allowing me the opportunity to help.

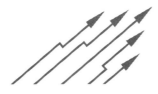

LOOKING FORWARD TO BOOK 3: HOW WILL IT BEGIN?

I have learned many interesting points since the release of Book 1 in April of 2019. One of the surprises was how positively the readers reacted to the use of my personal experiences as a way of introducing the various leadership lessons. It was as if the story aspect of the book took on a separate identity, almost like a book within a book. I received two particular messages loudly and clearly. There was one statement and one question: "Tell more stories," and "what happens next?"

In response, I have made a couple of changes going forward. First, I have added this final section to Book 2, sharing a portion of the first chapter of Book 3, titled *change to LIVE better & LEAD differently*, which is scheduled to be released in the spring of 2020. The other adjustment I have made is to the content of Book 3. Book 3 will be heavily weighted to the story side, even more than the first two books. I will still be including my original perspectives regarding change management and cultural transformation, but their presentation will be more intermixed with the life lesson stories. The sharing of life experiences will take center stage in Book 3.

Please find below a preview of Book 3's first story. It is a partial draft, but there is enough written for you to get a sense of the life lessons being learned.

Thank you and enjoy!

THE BEGINNING OF BOOK 3: I was standing in the hallway outside of Regional Bank's (RB) boardroom. I was waiting for the large, wooden double doors to open. There was a meeting already in progress inside the boardroom. It was running a little late and a handful of us were just milling around in the hall, waiting for the room to become available. Most of RB's executive leadership team were in the board-room participating in the investment committee meeting, which on this day was running over.

I was thirty-one or thirty-two years old at the time, depending on which month in 1989 this meeting actually took place. In either case, I had only been with RB for a couple months. Hired in as their account-ing manager, this was my first meeting with the assembled senior team. Prior to my joining RB, I had spent two years as a staff accountant in Global Resources Corporation's (GRC) Eastern Division Headquarters for the eastern part of the United States. At the time, GRC was one of America's 250 largest corporations. The Eastern Division of GRC focused on the exploration and production of oil and natural gas in sev-eral states. For those of you who know me from Books one and two, you already know that I was a leader in other industries prior to my entry into financial services, and you also know I would go on to lead several different organizations from health care to heavy construction. For those of you who don't know me, take a minute and review "Who is Rob?" at the end of this book. By the way, just as in the prior two books, my use of RB, GRC, and any other people or companies referenced in this book are not being referred to by their real names. The events are cer-tainly real. However, as was the case in my first two books *LIVE better LEAD differently* and *let's all LIVE better & LEAD differently*, I am choos-ing to put myself in the public eye, but I am not willing to subject others to the same exposure.

This meeting and the events that followed stand out clearly in my memory because of the life lessons rooted in these experiences. What makes them memorable? The emotion. The intense focus of the moment. The ability to recall with clarity a point in time where I was in the position to make a difference, learn a valuable lesson, or discover a truth. Each of these memorable lessons has helped me to develop the materials I shared with you in Books one and two, and those I am about to share with you now.

Returning to the RB hallway scene, I was pacing around for about ten minutes and making small talk with a couple other manager-level RB team members when the doors opened and out filed the investment committee members. No one acknowledged those of us standing in the hall because they were all still engaged in side conversations related to the previous meeting. After the boardroom was vacant, we went in, found an open seat, and waited for the missing RB executives to return. Before the meeting started, the chief information officer and the vice president of information technology joined us at the table. In about five minutes, all of the executive team had gathered. At the table, in addition to myself and those I have already mentioned, were RB's president and CEO, COO, CFO, EVP of HR, EVP of trust and investment operations, chief lending officers, EVP and corporate legal counsel, VP of internal audit, and the VP of marketing. The table was full. If you wanted to get something done, anything done within RB, this was the group you would want to gather.

I reported directly to the CFO. He had given me very specific instructions regarding when to speak, what to say, and to stay silent unless I was asked a direct question. If I was asked a question, I was to look to him to see if he wished to answer the question before I was permitted to respond. The information I was told to prepare for the meeting was also very tightly controlled and narrowly defined. I was not to hand out the information to anyone unless the CFO directed me to. I had no idea what the meeting was about. I just knew what I had been ordered to prepare. And, about that, the information I had with me had been reviewed and heavily edited by the CFO. He made multiple changes to the data, which materially altered the conclusions I had reached after doing the research. He explained to me that I clearly didn't understand the financial services industry. The CFO had been in banking his entire career, and his words to me when I questioned why he made the changes were: "I am a god when it comes to accounting. You just do what you are told!" I found his comments to be both incredibly insulting and wildly entertaining at the same time. I could even see them as being downright humorous if he hadn't been so serious. He actually believed that garbage. I will never forget that meeting. There were so many opportunities for me to observe human behavior and to learn from the experience.

In my short time with RB, I had learned much about the personalities of the executive team, especially the CFO. He had a very aggressive personality. It was "his way or the highway." Most of the executive team were cut from a similar cloth: very intelligent, high energy, in their forties and fifties, and in banking for their entire professional careers. Working in banking for your entire career is perfectly honorable, but in this case, their entire careers had been spent at only one bank, RB. They had already accumulated fifteen to twenty years of tenure within the organization and had climbed their way to the top within their respective divisions. Of those executives I had had a chance to directly observe, the CEO and the EVP of investment and trust were by far the most skilled leaders.

My background up to this point was very different from those seated at the table. Beginning at the age of nineteen, I had spent: four years in leadership within one of the nation's largest and fastest growing large-box, discount retailers; then three years selling copiers and office equipment on straight commission; followed by two years finishing my college degree with a major in accounting and finance; and another two years working as a staff accountant within Global Resources Corporation (one of America's 250 largest corporations). To say I perceived the world of business differently from the rest of the group would be an understatement. But, I was there to learn the financial services industry, and I <u>very</u> <u>much</u> needed this job, so I sat quietly and observed the proceedings with great interest.

I will save the specific topic of the meeting until the latter part of the story, simply for the effect of making my point. Once everyone was seated, the CEO opened the meeting by framing the strategic issue facing us on that day. RB had been approached by a much larger regional bank. This particular bank was one with which we already had multiple banking relations, so their contacting us regarding a joint venture opportunity was not unusual. They had proposed that our two companies work together and construct a different type of information technology (IT) platform in order to better serve our deposit customer base. The IT platform being proposed was one that the bigger bank had successfully put into service within several regional population centers. RB controlled over 50 percent of the deposit market share in its service area, so we were the logical choice to approach with this offer. (For those of you who are not familiar with the banking industry, a 25 percent market share for deposit volume in an area is very significant. RB's control over more than 50 percent of the deposit volume in our markets was huge. In our rural region of south central Ohio, RB was truly the eight hundred-pound-gorilla in banking.)

After the CEO framed the business proposal, the CIO weighed in offering his perspective. The CIO was completely against the idea and had a list of reasons as to why this idea would never work and would be a clear and present threat to the integrity of our IT systems. Sharing access to our proprietary programming would surely open a Pandora's box of pending disasters. He was certain that no one seated at the table could support such an unnecessary risk. Once he was finished demolishing the proposal, the other executives lined up in lockstep against the idea. The VP of IT spoke to the numerous difficulties and expenses related to upgrading our IBM mainframe computing platform to accommodate this new service, not to mention the additional programmers that would need to be hired just to keep up with the demands placed on the system by the proposed change.

Internal audit supported the concept of uncontrollable risk. The EVP of HR spoke to how tight we were in space in the IT area and how any increase in the number of programmers would require a remodeling of the entire IT area. Legal was skeptical of the contractual language, but thought they could work through the issues, given time. The VP of marketing saw no need for the addition of this new service to our current deposit-product offerings, especially when you considered the extra cost to RB and in light of all the risks being described. Then, it was time for the CFO to weigh in on the impact from all of these capital expenditures and operating expenses. Down the list of topics I had researched (and he had re-written) the CFO went. Each line item was becoming increasingly more dire and more prohibitive than the last, until finally, he looked in my direction. It was at this point the CFO introduced me to the group as the new accounting manager. He let them know that I did not have a banking background, but he thought that I could learn the "extremely complex business of banking" over time. He then said that I prepared the work he had just quoted, which was only true in the strictest sense. I did not appreciate being tagged as the person responsible for the information the CFO had just delivered to the group, but I sat quietly, letting the comment pass. Patience is a virtue, and I had learned long ago that in leadership as in life, timing is everything. Learn to wait for the right time.

Over the next twenty minutes, every other executive at the table, excluding the CEO and the EVP of trust and investment, added their reasons why this was a bad idea for RB and why it would never work. The consensus of those executives weighing in on the proposal was clear. The product would never catch on with the customer base and the costs/risks of entering into this new IT platform were just way too high for RB to even consider it. After all, we already had a 50 percent market share in our region, and this invitation was simply a way for the bigger regional bank to steal our customer base. The CEO then summarized the meeting by saying: "So, it is pretty clear. It is the consensus of the group that we need to reject the offer. Is there anyone in the room that thinks setting up the first Automated Teller Machine (ATM) network within our market is a good idea?"

Yes, that's right. This discussion was centered on the introduction of the first ATM network into the mostly rural markets we served. At the time this was being discussed by RB, it was a proven technology and had existed in the larger population centers for a few years. As I had researched the technology in preparation for the meeting, I had read about the initial start-up problems and costs, but the level of customer acceptance was exceptional. The problem for those seated at the table was it was simply different from what RB had done in the past. RB was the dominant force in our little corner of the state. "If it ain't broke, don't fix it." It is a wonderful strategic plan which has been the mantra of hundreds of companies, most of which are no longer in business.

During my tenure with GRC, the regional VP had, for whatever reason, taken a personal interest in my career. Several times over the prior couple of years, he had called me into his office and discussed the strategic direction of the eastern region as well as global GRC initiatives. This gentleman had been with GRC for several years more than I had been alive and was one of the corporation's most respected executives. One of the projects he asked me to work on was the global integration of GRC's management information system. This project was massive in scope and budget. It impacted almost every aspect of GRC's global operations from inventory tracking, to reserve projections, and to financial measurement and reporting. I had the pleasure of going to our world headquarters in Houston, Texas on multiple occasions and working with some of the company's best and brightest in the areas of IT and finance. Around the table in Houston, I had routinely heard from some of IBM's top systems design people and programmers. When financial options were discussed, it was done by one or more senior level partners from a big eight accounting and consulting firm. GRC's team members were also top-notch. They were highly recruited from all around the country and the world. Granted, around the GRC table, the numbers being thrown around had four or five more zeroes behind them than the RB numbers. It wasn't the difference in cost that stood out to me when I mentally compared the two meetings, but it was the difference in the leadership's attitude toward change.

The GRC project had dwarfed the RB proposal in every way imaginable: cost, complexity, and scope. Besides the difference in attitude toward change, what was particularly striking to me were the conclusions reached by RB's CIO regarding the computing platform required to support the proposed ATM network. Not six months earlier, I had witnessed the IBM engineers and technicians upgrade GRC's in-house IT system from the same basic platform RB was currently using to the new platform being requested to support the ATM network. The global upgrade was done without any major problems. I knew IBM was promoting these types of system upgrades across the country in all business environments. For RB's CIO to focus on system upgrade challenges, quoting IBM as his source for several of the concerns he listed, was surprising to me. I was also puzzled by his constant theme of ongoing security concerns. During the GRC project, security was also a constant topic. All of the voices around the table, internal and external, were focused on system integrity, and all GRC concerns had been addressed. The conclusions reached by RB's CIO were curious to me, as were the conclusions of the other executives that had spoken on the topic during the meeting. I had no way to know if they were wrong or GRC was right, or vice versa. I just knew what I had learned through my previous job experience, and I knew what I had read about the new ATM technology in my preparation for this meeting. None of what was going on around the RB table made any sense to me, and I could tell that the CEO was less than pleased regarding the conclusions being reached by his most senior leadership team.

Going back to the CEO's question to the assembled group: "Is there anyone in the room that thinks setting up the first Automated Teller Machine (ATM) network within our market is a good idea?" As soon as I heard the question, my hand shot up. It was a reflex action. When I looked around the table, mine was the only dissenting opinion being offered.

During most of my previous years of experience, senior leadership actually meant that question when they asked it. My thoughts, as well as anyone else's thoughts regarding the topic at hand, were always welcomed and encouraged. However, at this table, the only person interested in what I had to say was the CEO. Oh, my goodness, if looks could kill, I would have died many deaths in that moment. The CFO, in particular, was obviously not happy with my willingness to join the conversation. Hey, the man seated at the head of the table had just asked us a direct question, and I had a direct answer.

The CEO immediately acknowledged me. Before I began speaking, he welcomed me to the organization. He hoped that I would choose to make banking my career and that I would spend it with RB. Then he asked: "What is on your mind?" With that invitation, I gave a brief summary of my relevant experience with GRC and the global integration project I had been a part of. I was careful not to challenge anyone's conclusions directly, out of respect for those in the room and out of respect for the awesome power of corporate politics. Even though I was much younger than everyone else in the room, this wasn't my first high-level meeting, by any stretch. I knew from the looks and body language around the table that I was on very thin ice with almost all of the senior leadership team, and I needed to tread lightly. The focus of my comments was restricted to my familiarity with this type of conversion, the challenges faced, and the opportunities presented by re-considering this new technology. After all, taking another look at the project will cost very little, and I even offered the name and number of the lead engineer at IBM to our CIO if he wished to call him and discuss the issue.

When I stopped speaking, there was about a fifteen-second pause where you could have heard a pin drop on the carpeted floor. Then the room erupted. "Apples and oranges. Banking is way more complicated than oil and gas production!" "We don't have all the money in the world to spend on this project. No comparison!" Similar comments were hurled at me from every corner of the room, except one, the head of the table. The CEO had leaned back in his chair and was watching the spectacle unfold. Specifically, he was watching me as the spectacle unfolded. When I saw him looking at me, I made eye contact and gave him a slight grin, just enough to let him know that I knew a whole lot more about this type of meeting and this particular topic than he had been led to believe. The CEO let the blood-letting continue for about ten minutes. Then, with a calm tone, he brought the meeting to an abrupt close by saying: "Well clearly, we are not going to solve this issue here today. Let's meet early next week to finalize the decision. Rob, can I see you in my office please?" And with that, the meeting was over. The CEO was the first to leave the room. The CFO came over to me and said: "The minute he is done with you, I want you in my office!" The only other person that spoke to me after that meeting was the EVP of trust and investment. He came up to me with a big smile on his face, shook my hand, and said: "Welcome to RB!" You could tell this guy had been entertained by the fireworks, but he and I were the only two seated at the table that saw the humor in the situation.

I gathered my papers and made the short walk to the CEO's office. His administrative assistant asked me to take a seat in the reception area until Mr. E. (RB's CEO) was ready for me. In about five minutes, he emerged from his office with a big smile on his face, apologized for keeping me waiting, shook my hand, and asked: "So, how has your day gone so far?" Okay, now I knew there were three of us in the room that saw the humor in the situation.

He closed the door to his office behind us and asked me to be seated at the conference table in his office. "Well, that was interesting." These were the first words spoken by Mr. E., setting the tone for that meeting and for my career that followed. (Welcome to Book 3! …To be continued…)

WHO IS ROB?

Based on my reading of many leadership books, it is customary for the author to provide information about themself to the reader. Okay, I guess this is as good a time as any to tell you a little bit about me. I have been truly blessed both with family and career.

I was born in Elyria, OH, in 1958 and lived in a couple different communities outside of Cleveland, OH, through the second grade. In 1967, Dad accepted a new job and our family of five moved to a small community in central West Virginia. In 1968, we relocated to a remote farm in central WV, which is where I grew up through high school graduation. I was the youngest of three children. Mom and Dad lived on that same farm and loved it until they passed away.

My wife of thirty-nine years deserves all the credit for what we have been able to accomplish together. We have one son. He is a civil engineer, who went on to earn his master's in management and has attained his PE certification. At the time I am writing this book, he and our daughter-in-law have been married for over six years. My wife holds a bachelor's degree in education. My formal education is a bachelor's degree in business administration with an accounting/finance major.

Over the course of my career, I have held various levels of responsibility, including but not limited to the following positions: chairman of the board of directors, chief executive officer, president, chief financial officer, chief administrative officer, chief innovation officer, executive vice president, vice president of finance, controller, etc. I have held these levels of responsibility while leading (teaching) within six different industries, including: large box retail, direct, commission-based sales, global development of natural resources, regional financial services, health care administration, and large project construction. These organizations spanned a range of ownership structures from privately held to publicly traded and from companies that were very much for profit to organizations with the tax designation of not-for-profit. I have attained multiple certifications in disciplines which include: leadership, sales, total quality management, re-engineering, and most recently, a lean practitioner.

As a leader within these differing organizations, my strategic objectives have varied, but I can summarize them for you by providing this brief list: turn struggling companies around while achieving financial and cultural stability; manage all aspects of accretive, sustainable growth, including growth by mergers and acquisitions; and leading cultural transformation resulting in enhanced, sustainable franchise value. In short, I have spent the majority of my leadership career as the person held accountable for positive results, and I am okay with that.

I have been a student of leadership and an observer of human nature my entire career. I enjoy the challenges of building an organization, and I love the process of helping others to grow. Believe me when I tell you that I am nothing special. I am a product of hard work and hard knocks. If I can succeed by applying the concepts presented in this book, you can succeed by applying the same concepts. To summarize, my purpose is pretty straightforward. I am here to help and I am grateful for every opportunity to do so.

That's pretty much it. It is my deepest hope that you have found value in these pages and that I have been able to help you in some small way.

My thanks to you for providing me with a continuous opportunity to teach.

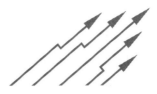

ACKNOWLEDGMENTS

I was the person at the keyboard putting these words onto the page, but with me stood a cast of hundreds which have helped me along the way. Allow me to begin by saying "Thank you" to the literary team, Larry Carpenter along with Clovercroft Publishing, without whom I would have never been able to take these words from the computer to the market.

My thanks to Jana and Jody at Maxwell Studios for the photography.

Website design and development, "LIVEbetterLEADdifferentlybooks. com", have been created by Bricks Without Straw. Thanks to Jamie and his team for all of their work.

My mom and dad have been gone for several years. They shaped much of what I am today, and for that, I will always be grateful. A little over a year ago, Jennifer lost her mother. She was a second mother to me. I love her and I will always carry her with me.

During the drafting process for Book 2, the input and perspective gained from my family was absolutely critical. Adam, Julie, Pam, and Dixie, to all of you, I am very grateful for your guidance. Thank you! I hope you are up for Book 3.

There was one person outside of my family that was key in helping me with the creative process, Sarah. Sarah is an accomplished executive and a very talented leader in her own right. From the earliest stages of Book 1 and through all of Book 2, Sarah encouraged me to share more of my personal experiences. She kept me focused on providing a more meaningful context for the reader. THANK YOU for your friendship, your patience, and your guidance!

Which brings me to the most important person of all, my wonderful wife of thirty-nine years, Jennifer. Without her support and encouragement, these books and a lifetime of experience would have not been possible. THANK YOU for everything I am and for all that we will experience together in the future. I am the luckiest guy in the world!